Matthew A. Henson's
Historic Arctic Journey

Matthew A. Henson's Historic Arctic Journey

The Classic Account of One of the World's Greatest Black Explorers

MATTHEW A. HENSON

FOREWORD BY ROBERT E. PEARY,
REAR ADMIRAL, U.S.N.
INTRODUCTIONS BY DEIRDRE C. STAM
AND BOOKER T. WASHINGTON

THE LYONS PRESS
Guilford, Connecticut
An Imprint of the Globe Pequot Press

Copyright © 2009 Morris Book Publishing, LLC

Reprinted from the 1912 edition published as *A Negro Explorer at the North Pole* by Frederick Stokes, New York. Three photographs and an appendix have been dropped from that edition.

The Lyons Press is an imprint of The Globe Pequot Press.

Text design: Sheryl Kober
Layout Artist: Kim Burdick
Project Manager: David Legere

Library of Congress Cataloging-in-Publication Data is available on file.

ISBN 978-1-59921-308-8

Printed in the United States of America

10 9 8 7 6 5 4 3 2 1

Table of Contents

ACKNOWLEDGMENTS

Honoring Mathew Henson during this centennial year is a privilege for The Explorers Club. In republishing his autobiography, we celebrate in Matthew Henson characteristics admired in an explorer—courage, endurance, and great dignity.

This edition is Volume V of The Explorers Club Classics Series. Support and encouragement for this project came from EC president Daniel Bennett; Ronald Rosner, chairman of the Library/Archives Committee; Elysa Engelman of The Mystic Seaport Museum, who arranged for the photographing of our Henson artifacts on loan to the museum; Dorthea Sartain, EC curator of collections; and her predecessor, Clare Flemming, who suggested that we republish *A Negro Explorer at the North Pole*. Clare also introduced us to scholars Deirdre C. Stam, who graciously gave of her time to write a new introduction for this edition, and David H. Stam, who prepared the bibliography. The EC is grateful also to Susan Kaplan and Anne Witty of the Peary-MacMillan Arctic Museum of Bowdoin College, who generously shared their time and expertise with us. And finally, the EC wishes to thank Syracuse University for assistance with photography.

Once again The Explorers Club has benefited from our association with The Lyons Press. Our editor there, Holly

Rubino, understood the Club's close association with Matthew Henson and the importance of this centennial occasion.

— LINDLEY KIRKSEY YOUNG
The Explorers Club Imprint, April 23, 2008

Introduction to The Explorers Club Edition

Why are we interested in Matthew Henson as we enter the centennial year of the great North Pole controversy? The ostensible reason is that Henson served as an essential figure—driver of dogs, translator of Inuktitut, skilled jack-of-all-trades, and a man of exceptional strength, courage, and endurance—during Robert E. Peary's daring and famous attempts to reach the North Pole culminating in the notable journey of 1909. But skilled and loyal assistants on other polar ventures, however famous the expedition and its leader, are seldom remembered and rarely celebrated. The answer probably lies as much in recent American social history as in the narrow field of polar history. Matthew Henson has served in the popular imagination, not only as standard-bearer for American geographic attainments, as has Peary himself, but also as symbol of bravery and physical prowess by a person of African-American ancestry in the challenging field of polar exploration.

When weighing the achievements of Peary and Henson over six voyages and eighteen years in the Far North, we must always keep in mind the extreme conditions faced by these intrepid venturers. Traveling to Ellesmere Island, the northwest coast of Greenland, and the Arctic Ocean, they encountered ferocious winds and storms, shifting and unstable ice, jagged surfaces, long periods of depressing darkness, and

intensely cold temperatures. These impediments affected
not only their physical progress but, as happens with all such
expeditions, also their judgment and decision making during their six expeditions. Aware of the physical difficulties, we
generally avoid arm-chair criticism here and instead celebrate
the considerable human achievement of the Peary-Henson
collaboration in northern exploration.

The value of Matthew Henson to Peary's expeditions is
well recognized. In an oft-quoted phrase, Peary said of Henson: "I can't get along with out him." Elaborating, Peary claimed
that Henson "can handle a sledge better, and is probably a better dog-driver, than any other man living, except some of the
best of the Eskimo hunters themselves."[1] Another member of
the famous 1909 expedition, Donald MacMillan, in the 1920
edition of *National Geographic* described Henson with these
words: "He was indispensable to Peary and of more real value
than the combined services of all four white men. . . . With
years of experience equal to that of Peary himself, an expert
dog driver, a master mechanic, physically strong and most
popular with the Eskimos, talking the language like a native,
clean, full of grit, he went to the pole with Peary because he
was easily the most efficient of all Peary's assistants."

Though no one served longer with Peary than Henson,
there were other people on Peary's expeditions who enjoyed
more status at the time and were equally brave and resourceful, but are known today only among dedicated enthusiasts of

polar history. Yet it is the name of Matthew Henson, who died in 1955 at eighty-eight, that has survived with a reasonable degree of recognition into the twenty-first century among readers of all ages. Among young Americans reading about the discovery of the North Pole, it is quite possible that Matthew Henson's name is better known than that of the expedition leader, Peary himself. Why is this so?

Controversy, of course, can enhance fame, if not reputation. And Henson was controversial, though more through circumstances than by intent. While Henson's skills, physical courage, and stamina on the trail were generally recognized, the interpretation of his role on that famous last journey has given rise to much comment and even dispute. The salient point for many has been the matter of race. At the time of Peary's "conquest" of the North Pole in 1909, questions arose about whether Henson—as a person of African ancestry, whom Peary repeatedly described as a servant—could be and should be accorded at least the moderate recognition that was granted to the Caucasian members of the polar party. Later, when details of the exploit were presented to a curious public, the question arose as to whether it was Peary, the partially disabled organizer and leader of the party, or Henson, the principal sledge driver and effectively Peary's most constant companion and steadfast assistant, who actually stepped first on that supposedly magical patch of ice that Peary identified as the site of the North Pole.

Henson became further embroiled in controversy when Dr. Frederick A. Cook, who had been with Peary on the Greenland trip of 1891–1892, claimed that he had reached the pole first by a year, thus putting both Peary and Henson out of the running altogether for this signal honor. Henson, respected for his ability to speak Inuktitut, participated in translating the testimony of Eskimos who had traveled with Cook, and Henson's subsequent comments, or perhaps lack of them, seemed to affirm Peary's claim of primacy above that of Cook's. Henson has been criticized both for what he said and what he did not say about the substance of that interview.

Henson was the focus for the race-tinged question of why Peary chose Henson and not the experienced Robert Bartlett, the last white man to be sent back on the final 1909 dash to the pole. Was it, as Peary's critics charged, so that Peary would have no credible witness to his hoax? Peary gave these reasons for his choice: Henson would not have the skills to lead the return party should Peary have been lost; Henson was the best man for the sledging work beside the Eskimos, who with their "racial inheritance of ice technics" were more necessary to him than any white man; Henson was skillful with dogs and sledges; and Peary wanted to "give Henson some return" for his faithful service.[2]

Finally, Henson charged Peary with inexplicably and cruelly shunning him, his longtime traveling companion, from the moment the flag was planted on the "pole," and all but cutting off contact with him shortly after arriving back in the

United States, despite his oft-cited public praise of Henson's skills and loyalty in earlier years. While *shunning* may be too strong a word, it is true that Peary was angry with Henson for attempting to cash in on his polar exploits through publications and a lecture tour, though it may be that Henson did not sign the agreements to which the other expedition party members agreed, allowing Peary all rights of publicity. Whatever the truth of the matter, the estrangements fed the controversy. Was the distance caused by Henson's transgressions of post-expedition etiquette, as Peary noted in personal documents, or by Peary's own insatiable desire for public recognition as the "First Man to Reach the North Pole"?

What the public mainly remembers today is that Matthew Henson was a person of African ancestry (and more significantly a descendant of free people in the American South) who participated in essential ways in the most famous attempts by an American party to be the first to reach the North Pole. In shorthand fashion, Henson has been credited in print, with language changing over the years, as: the first Negro (or later black man, or African American) to travel to the North Pole; or the first man, at all, to reach the Pole; or the first American to reach the pole; or as one of the first scientists or geographers of his race. The many accounts are quite formulaic, consisting of a tale of rags-to-adventure-to-obscurity-to-overdue-appreciation. All draw the essence of the story from Henson's own autobiography, the text of which constitutes the major part of this volume.

THE AUTOBIOGRAPHY

Henson's own account of his twenty-three years with Peary, published in 1912 as *A Negro Explorer at the North Pole*,[3] has been generally accepted as an accurate representation of that period of time from the author's perspective, although it departs in several details from Peary's *The North Pole*. This work is reproduced here with the title *Matthew A. Henson's Historic Arctic Journey: The Classic Account of One of the World's Greatest Black Explorers*.

The first edition included a foreword by "R. E. Peary" and an introduction by Booker T. Washington, both reproduced in this edition. Henson's text, which makes up the central part of this volume, is basically a factual account, detailing the daily activity, survival techniques, adventures, and accomplishments of the expedition. Henson describes the various command structures under which he worked without comment or question, and his descriptions constantly reinforce the primary role of Peary as the major force behind all decisions and undertakings. In this work Henson is modest about his own role.

In describing his function on Peary-led expeditions, Henson represents himself simply as a man among other men, each of whom had clearly defined roles. His was that of general assistant, skilled craftsperson, interpreter, and laborer. Others, with more formal education but in most cases less clearly applicable skills, enjoyed a collegiality among themselves to which he had access, but not on fully equal terms. Henson does not dwell upon the reasons for his subordinate position—be they educational background, prior social status, or race. He refers only obliquely to race in his concluding remarks[4] with the quotation, "Now is Othello's occupation gone." One imagines that this work in its first appearance could have been marketed accurately and simply as a polar adventure by "one who has been there."

From the beginning, however, Henson's book was placed in the context of race. The title, of course, with *Negro* (or, in later editions of 1969 and 1989, *black*) as initial qualifier to *explorer,* sends a message to the reader that the novelty lies in the author's racial identity among pursuers of this romantic activity. Two introductory sections reinforce this emphasis. In the foreword, Robert Peary provides what he seems to intend as a laudatory statement: "The example and experience of Matthew Henson . . . is only another one of the multiplying illustrations of the fact that race, or color, or bringing-up, or environment, count nothing against a determined heart, if it is backed and aided by intelligence. Henson proved his fitness by long and thorough apprenticeship, and his participation in the final victory which planted the Stars and Stripes at the North Pole . . . is a distinct credit and feather in the cap of his race." Drawing from a text Peary had prepared for a dinner honoring Henson sponsored by the National Association for the Advancement of Colored People (NAACP) in 1909, he further notes, "I congratulate you and your race upon

Matthew Henson. . . . He should be an everlasting example to your young men that these qualities [loyalty, persistence, and endurance] will win whatever object they are directed at." Peary goes on to say, "Henson, son of the tropics, has proven through years, his ability to stand tropical, temperate, and the fiercest stress of frigid, [sic] climate and exposure."

The original publisher's decision to have Booker T. Washington write an introduction reinforces the reader's impression that Henson's race is the significant factor of the account, and specifically the novelty of a traveler of African ancestry in the Far North. Washington begins by asking how it came about that "besides the four Esquimos, Matt Henson, a Negro, was the only man to whom was accorded the honor of accompanying [Peary] on the final dash to the goal." To answer this question, Washington quotes "in substance" from Peary. Here is Washington's restatement of Peary's argument: "Matthew Henson, my Negro assistant, has been with me in one capacity or another since my second trip to Nicaragua in 1887 . . . This position I have given him primarily because of his adaptability and fitness for the work and secondly on account of his loyalty." These are, of course, attributes of a follower, not a leader. Washington goes on to praise the "faithful service" that made Henson indispensable, and to praise Peary as "not only willing to accept the service but . . . at the same time generous enough to acknowledge it." Washington notes that Henson's story proves "again that courage, fidelity, and ability are honored and rewarded under a black skin as well as under a white."[5] Even at the time of his writing, Washington, then principal of the Tuskegee Normal and Industrial Institute, was under attack for overvaluing the qualities of submission, loyalty, tenacity, and ceaseless effort for people of African ancestry in their quest for a better place in early-twentieth-century American society. He placed Henson's book in the tradition of the inspirational account of a "faithful servant."

Henson himself addressed race with equanimity in the book itself: "From the building of the pyramids and the journey to the Cross, to the discovery of the new world and the discovery of the North Pole, the Negro had been the faithful and constant companion of the Caucasian, and I felt all that it was possible for me to feel, that it was I, a lowly member of my race, who had been chosen by fate to represent it, at this, almost the last of the world's great *work*."[6]

Though usually described as an "autobiography," *Negro Explorer at the North Pole* is almost exclusively an account of Henson's participation in Peary's Arctic ventures with emphasis on the final expedition, that of 1909 to the North Pole. Henson's account attests to the imagination, courage, preparation, ingenuity, strength, and energy demonstrated by almost all in Peary's party. It does so only indirectly, however, by calmly setting forth the facts of the journeys, illuminating them with telling and lively detail. He rarely uses the hyperbolic language of the contemporary press and other explorers, who favored the terminology of military victory: *winning, achieving, accomplishing,* and *subduing.* Henson often praises and rarely criticizes other members of the expedition. A rare exception to his positive tone is found in his description of Frederick A. Cook's lack of skills in the field. Henson is reticent, however, on his own contributions to the larger goal. Whether this tone of the work indicates Henson's innate modesty, or his loyalty to Peary, or Peary's influence of the content of the book, or Henson's response to the demands of a publisher with an eye to the market, is a question that can probably never be answered.

Some have suggested that the autobiography does not represent Henson's work at all but was ghostwritten because Henson was effectively illiterate.[7] Given the extent of controversy over the matter, one must address the questions of whether Henson could, at a basic level, read and write.

There are strong indications that Henson had good reading skills. Some come from his own statements, such as his crediting Captain Childs with teaching him when he was a cabin boy. There is evidence that he worked on reading and writing also with Dr. Thomas S. Dedrick, Peary's expedition surgeon, who makes a note to this effect in his diary of 1900.[8] As for his general reading, Henson mentions books at several points in the autobiography of 1912 and in Bradley Robinson's *Dark Companion,* a work representing Henson's retrospection as he worked with the author some thirty-five years later. In the last trip, for example, Henson notes that he had in his cabin Dickens's *Bleak House,* Kipling's *Barrack*

Room Ballads, poems of Thomas Hood, the Holy Bible, and Peary's books *Northward Over the Great Ice* and *Nearest the Pole.* According to Pauline Angell, Henson saw the phrase "Matthew A. Henson, my body servant" in Peary's book and "closed the book with a bang, gave it another with his fist, dropped it on the floor, and kicked it away."[9] In the unsourced account by Angell (to which Henson is credited as contributing), Henson is described as referring to Sairy Gamp in *Martin Chuzzlewit,* though the reference could have come from hearing the book read aloud and not necessarily from direct reading.[10] Additionally, there are numerous references to Henson's using notes for his post-1909 lecture tour, and there exists a videotape of his reading the first few words from a document during an awards ceremony in his last years.[11] Early in his speech, however, Henson was overcome by emotion and ceased his reading.

As for Henson's technical writing skills, the most convincing evidence consists of five documents handwritten and signed by Henson, now in the National Archives and Records Administration (NARA).[12] These show a large, well-formed script, lightly inscribed, with a phonetic approach to spelling. Most were written when Henson had no possible access to help from home. Punctuation is almost entirely absent. Though not adhering to formal English, Henson's spelling and grammar are consistent in themselves across documents and conform to a regional dialect. An edited transcript of an interview by Lowell Thomas with Matthew Henson, published in 1939, reinforces the impression of Henson's use of language that one gets from his early, handwritten letters. The language is direct and reads much like spoken English. The writer's meaning is entirely clear.

By contrast, there are some dedicatory inscriptions and typewritten letters signed by Henson in the MacMillan archives of Bowdoin College and at The Explorer's Club from a much later period that exhibit a grasp of standard style and grammar. Their language is rather more indirect. It is possible that these later letters, though generally similar in tone to the early epistles, were typed and edited by Henson's wife, Lucy Ross, who was an accomplished businesswoman and a member of several professional societies. Her penmanship and grammatical conventions, as shown in a letter from her to the Explorers Club after her husband's death, are quite similar to some of Henson's later letters that bear his signature. It should be noted that some of the letters written in Henson's later life to MacMillan exhibit his large, looped script—which appears on signed documents at NARA—but those to Mac-Millan show sophisticated grammar and spelling, and with occasional penned corrections and strikeovers. It is possible that in the handwritten letters to MacMillan, Henson was copying from drafts that had been corrected, if not fully created, for this purpose by his wife. Unscrambling this ambiguous evidence is not easy. It is perhaps safe to say that while Henson could read and write, and he could craft the basic prose for an appropriate communication, he probably relied heavily on an editor, most likely his wife Lucy, to help him with his correspondence. This seems a reasonable arrangement for the pair in light of their varying styles and skills. Henson could be talkative and charming in private conversation; Lucy was the more careful, even questioning and sometimes suspicious. She may have functioned as a protector of Henson's reputation, strategically shaping his message when she thought it necessary.[13]

That still begs the question of authorship of the volume. Henson made no secret of his wife's participation in his writing endeavors, the autobiography among them. On April 10, 1911, Henson wrote to Peary, "I am writing to ask a favor of you which I sincerely hope will be granted. My wife and I are writing a book and would like very much to have you write a preface."[14] Despite this reference, it is still possible that the autobiography was ghostwritten, as opposed simply to being edited by his publisher, Frederick A. Stokes.

Here, too, the evidence is complex. It was a principle of the Stokes firm, Henson's publisher, to allow "Freedom for the author ... if criticism or suggestion is offered this is done with the thought of helping the author to a better realization of his own conception."[15] This approach seems to have been used here. On July 29, 1911, Stokes wrote to Peary, "regarding the Henson book ... In general, it seems to me best not to attempt to polish the work much, but merely to omit anything that is too strong. I think that the book will be much more interesting if left as nearly as possible in the form in which Henson

wrote it, with all its defects, as to revise this away would be
to destroy the straight-forwardness, sincerity, and personality
shown."[16] In a letter written on January 10, 1965, regarding
authorship of *Negro Explorer at the North Pole*—half a century
after the fact—Donald MacMillan states his belief to Irene
Faunce of the Houghton Mifflin Company that "the book
was not written by Matt himself but by an assistant of Frederick A. Stokes and Company."[17] This assertion is repeated by
Rear Admiral Thomas D. Davies in 1989.[18] No ghostwriter for
Henson is named, however. By contrast, the name of Peary's
ghostwriter of *The North Pole*, A. E. Thomas, was relatively
well known. Peary's work, like Henson's, was published by the
Stokes Company.

What appears in the autobiography could very well be a
fair representation of Henson's language and, to some degree,
his prose. That is not to say that some, or even much, edit-
ing did not take place, either by his wife or by his publisher.
As for organization of material, there, too, it is quite possible
that an editor's skills were brought to bear, as was and still
is typical for most "autobiographies" by persons whose main
accomplishments are other-than-literary. What Henson did
say in his autobiography, in the main, is consistent with what
he said in various ways over the rest of his life, though with
some embroidery in later years.

Henson is careful to state throughout his autobiography
that he kept a diary upon which, by implication, his book was
based. Here are just a few examples of this contention. "From

my diary, the first entry since leaving the land; with a couple of comments added afterward."[19] Other references sprinkle the autobiography: "This from my log,"[20] "while the tea is brewing I am using the warmth to write,"[21] and, about Cook, "I will quote from my diary the impressions noted in regard to him."[22] And again, referring to his description of the last expedition of the Peary Arctic Club, Henson explained, "I did endeavor to keep a diary or journal of daily events, and did not find it difficult aboard the ship . . . but I found it impossible to make daily entries while in the field, on account of the constant necessity of concentrating my attention on the real business of the expedition."[23]

No trace of that diary has in fact been found, although there are a few loose, diary-like pages in Henson's hand, dated 1905, in the NARA collections. It is possible that Peary, who demanded to have the diaries of all of the participants on his expeditions, acquired that document at some time, but it has not been found with the other caches of Peary's materials. Henson's reference to that diary throughout the autobiography suggests that he had it, or some kind of written record, in hand at least during the three years after returning from the pole, while the autobiography published in 1912 was in preparation. Whether the "diary" was an actual document guiding the creation of the autobiography, or a literary conceit, remains a mystery. Robert M. Bryce, a scholar of Peary–Henson travels, claims that Henson's memory of the facts of the final North Pole trek was at least influenced by the diaries and publications of others, such as the diary of Dr. John Goodsell, Peary's surgeon in 1908–1909, and Peary's *The North Pole*.[24]

Bryce also contends that Peary himself played a role in determining the content of Henson's book so that it be consistent with his own account. In this interpretation, it was Peary who initially asked the publisher, Frederick A. Stokes, to publish the work; Peary even offered to insure Stokes against loss. Stokes demurred but was willing to accept $500 for "advertising." Both Peary and Stokes had the right to edit the manuscript. Some changes were suggested by Peary but never made.[25]

Henson's later retelling in articles and interviews of critical events in the 1908–1909 trip includes significant variations on the versions in the autobiography. In most retellings, Henson takes considerably more credit for essential actions and achievements. Some critics have questioned Henson's veracity, but others ascribe the variations to the need to provide "a good story" for the media, invoking the privileges of the oral and storytelling traditions. We should remember that by the time Henson received considerable attention from the mainstream press, he was an old man and as such should be accorded the privileges of a garrulous recounting.

Henson's oral style comes out in a rare bit of film footage of an interview with him in his eighties.[26] It suggests that he was a thoughtful, soft-spoken, polite man, who was somewhat uncomfortable with the attention given him. Of his radio and television experiences, Henson said in an interview,

"I don't like that microphone. . . . I'd rather be face to face with a polar bear."[27] Still of compact and wiry build,[28] Henson's impish humor is evident in his cryptic but nonetheless polite responses.

HENSON'S LIFE AMPLIFIED

Although the basic facts of Henson's life are not generally disputed, the details in various early accounts are not entirely consistent. The best information is from two sources: Henson's autobiography, of course, and Robinson's *Dark Companion*. When drawing information from these accounts, the reader must keep in mind the widely separated publication dates of the two works, as well as their different basic authorship arrangements. Both were designed to sell, of course, but the authors' purposes in telling the story differed. The autobiographical work of 1912 carried the weight of solidifying the primacy claim shortly after the return of Peary's party to the United States. It also bore the burden of convincing a skeptical public, brought up on myths of racial climatic inevitability, that a person of African-American background could perform effectively, even heroically, in the intense cold of the icy regions. The emphasis of the autobiography was on the facts of the journey.

Robinson's *Dark Companion* might be considered, by contrast, instructive entertainment and fictional biography combined, with invented dialogue added to clarify the message for a contemporary audience. An example of Robinson's creativity with a moral, according to Lyle Dick, is the imagined discussion, with no accompanying footnotes, around the incident of Peary's frozen toes, where the degree of Henson's involvement in the amputation varies with the telling.[29] Although explorer MacMillan's foreword for *Dark Companion* implies an endorsement, in fact MacMillan asked for many corrections that were not made. MacMillan was particularly irked at what he considered the overstatement of Henson's role in the expedition when he saw that the subtitle "Co-discoverer of the North Pole" had been added after he had seen the proposed text.[30]

This is the story that the reader takes from the combined sources. Matthew Henson was born on August 8, 1866, in Charles County, Maryland, to a family of freeborn sharecroppers of African-American descent. His mother died when Matthew Henson was two years old. His father, Lemuel, soon married his third wife, who was cruel to the child. Henson's father died in about 1874. His ancestry is generally unknown except for a possible link to Josiah Henson, generally considered the model for Harriet Beecher Stowe's Uncle Tom.

The boy left his extended family either at age seven, according to *Dark Companion,* or at about eleven, according to his autobiography. In either case, he had a scant six years of formal schooling. From seven to eleven, he probably joined an uncle in Washington, DC, where he attended the N Street School. In the more colorful version of his life in *Dark*

Companion, Henson, after leaving home, was given shelter, or at least work, by Janey Moore, who operated Janey's Home-Cooked Meals Cafe. There he supposedly met local sailor and runaway slave Baltimore Jack, who inspired him to go to sea. Whatever the sequence and dates, at about age twelve the young Matt found a post as cabin boy aboard the *Katie Hines* under the command of Captain Childs, who educated the boy informally in literature, mathematics, and navigation.[31] After Childs's death, probably in December 1883, Henson left the *Katie Hines* for odd jobs in Boston, Providence, Buffalo, and New York. In the following few years, he found employment as a seaman and traveled widely.

Of this youthful biographical detail, Sheldon N. Ripley, who was preparing another biography of Henson in 1964, noted in a letter to Robinson that he could not find sources for some details.[32] Specifically Ripley queried assertions about the cause of death for Henson's father, the reference to Janey Moore's restaurant, Henson's walking to Baltimore as a young boy to find a job as cabin boy, his leaving a poorly managed ship in Newfoundland, and his working as a stock boy in Washington, DC. Ripley's publisher received assurance from Henson's widow that these details were accurate, and they were included in Ripley's juvenile biography.[33]

At age nineteen, Henson returned to Washington, where he eventually found work as a clerk in a store owned by B. H. Steinmetz and Sons. There, in 1887, he fortuitously met Peary, a customer preparing for a second surveying trip to Nicaragua.

Peary immediately engaged him as "body-servant," according to Henson. Once in Nicaragua, the young man soon began assisting Peary with "chain work" and other tasks relating to surveying. After the pair returned to the United States, Henson probably went back to Steinmetz, but he soon had a new job. In 1889–1891, Peary helped arrange a job for Henson running errands and serving as a messenger in his office at the League Island Naval Yard in Philadelphia. Henson was then twenty-two and Peary, thirty-two.

In 1890 Peary organized his second trip to Greenland, with Henson among the crew. After returning to the United States, Henson married Eva Flint in 1891, but the pair divorced in 1897 after Henson suspected that his wife's affections had been directed elsewhere during his absence. A poignant, handwritten (undated) letter from Henson to Peary explaining this situation and seeking his understanding can be found in the National Archives collections. Soon afterward Henson joined Peary, Peary's new wife Josephine, and others for another expedition to the North.

Peary and Henson spent time together on six forays to Greenland, with the last culminating in the 1909 attempt to reach the North Pole. Henson was paid little during these trips, earning between $25 and $35 monthly for all but the last, when he may have received $50 a month as well as a bonus.[34]

Both Henson and Peary lived intimately with Eskimo women during their years in Greenland, and both fathered sons whom they essentially abandoned after leaving Greenland in 1909. The boys were raised in their mothers' and stepfathers' tight-knit families. Henson's son with Akatingwah was Ahnahkaq (or Anaukaq).[35] Henson's good relations with the Eskimos who supported Peary's parties are well known and a staple of the Henson story. MacMillan goes so far as to say that Henson lived more often with Eskimos than with the white members of the expeditions, thus "their liking for and their faith in him."[36] It is not surprising that Henson felt more comfortable with these companions than with the Pearys and some other regular members of the expedition. Peary clearly indicated his desire to maintain social distance and administrative hierarchy. In diary notes preparatory to a talk with Henson on managerial matters when the two were at Fort Conger, Peary outlines what he intends to say on the subject of organizational discipline.[37] From the context of the notes, it seems that Peary was troubled by some sense of challenge to his leadership at this time and felt the need to have special meeting with Henson to reestablish greater formality in their relationship.

> *Am old enough now & you have been*
> *in my service long enough to show me more*
> *respect in small things. Have a right to*
> *expect you will say sir to me always. That*
> *you will pay attention when I am talking*
> *to you & show that you hear the directions*
> *I give you by saying yes, sir, or all right, sir.*

Have no fault to find when we are alone together but when Dr or number of us present or we are on board ship you are very different. Will give you memorandum of this.

Mrs. Peary's attitude toward Henson, who joined her husband and party during three trips to the Far North (1891–1892, 1893–1895, and 1900), can be inferred from the nature of her many references to him in her book on the first trip, *My Arctic Journal.* Throughout the work she refers to him as "Matt" even as she calls the other men in the party by more formal appellations: Mr. Peary, Dr. Cook, Verhoeff, Astrup, and Gibson. While "Matt" could be her "steady guardian," he is most often the one who cooks, or cleans up, or performs other menial tasks.[38] Josephine Peary does make an effort to celebrate Henson's birthday,[39] as is done for each member of the expedition, and she expresses sympathy at one point for his "grippe"—but in general she pays little attention to him as a person. Probably reflecting family attitudes, the Pearys' daughter Marie referred to Henson dismissively as "practically uneducated."[40] Josephine herself in later years labeled Henson a "vainglorious braggart," no doubt protecting her husband's reputation as the ultimate "first" in all claims relating to the North Pole.[41]

Despite occasional irritations on both sides, Peary and Henson seem to have worked compatibly during their polar years. In 1893, for example, Peary named Cape Henson in northwest Greenland (77°23' North latitude; 71°18' longitude) in Henson's honor. From 1891 through 1902, Peary, with Henson at his side, explored several areas of Greenland, mapped the north coast using Fort Conger as his base from 1898 on, and attempted to find a way over the Arctic ice and waters to the Pole. After 1902, Peary was preoccupied with raising funds for a ship of his own design to carry his next party to the Northeast Coast of Ellesmere Island. While not working with Peary, Henson, to support himself, traveled through parts of the United States as a railroad porter. In 1897 he worked briefly as assistant to the curator who was preparing an Arctic display at the American Museum of Natural History (AMNH) in New York. This institution was the recipient of some Greenlandic objects from Peary's expeditions, including three meteorites, contents of Eskimo graves, and other examples of material culture. In early 1898 Henson again had contact with the AMNH when he was called to translate for the ailing Eskimos, among them the child Minik (or Mene), who had been brought to that institution by Peary for purposes of study at the request of Franz Boas.[42]

In 1905 Peary took his new vessel, the SS *Roosevelt,* north. Assisted by Henson, Bob Bartlett, and Ross Marvin, he made another attempt to reach the North Pole in early 1906. This time his party was stopped by a six-day blizzard and widening leads in the ice and had to turn back at 84°30'N. In 1908 he took the thoroughly overhauled *Roosevelt* to Cape Sheridan at the northern tip of Ellesmere Island and transferred twenty-four men and supplies to Cape Columbia. From there in March 1909, he headed north toward the Pole. On the final stage of this last attempt in late March and early April, Peary was accompanied by five men, Henson and four Eskimos. Peary announced the success of his journey, first from Indian Harbour and later from Battle Harbour, Labrador, from which the party returned to the United States; Henson and Peary then went their separate ways. The latter was soon preoccupied with defending his claim to primacy at the pole against Frederick Cook's rival claim for that honor.

On his return from the last voyage, Henson initially suffered from the aftereffects of snow blindness and was provided with temporary housing by Dr. Frederick Cook, who also arranged for his medical care. Henson was sustained financially during this period by the final payment from the Peary Arctic Club of the $750 promised to all members of the famous expedition. Additionally there was a bonus, variously described as $150 or $1,000. About this final payment, Peary was worried that Henson might consider it a bribe to support the expedition leader in the controversies surrounding his claim to primacy. Peary wrote to his backer Herbert Bridgman, "I would not have him [Henson] get the idea that I am endeavoring to do anything for him or that I am trying to get solid, or any allied idea for a thousand dollars. He has deliberately and premeditatedly deceived me and I am done with him absolutely." The context suggests that it was Henson's lecture tour that particularly irritated Peary, but the writer does not specify his particular point of contention. Peary and Henson met only twice after their return to the United States in 1909.[43]

Peary, as leader of this historic expedition, basked immediately in adulation from his grateful backers and an admiring public. Cook, too, was accorded public notice in their bitter competition, but he soon lost out to Peary in the struggle for recognition and reward. Henson and white members of Peary's party shared little of the limelight. The Eskimos of either expedition experienced no public acclaim at all.

Henson's financial situation at this time was particularly difficult. Against Peary's wishes, he attempted a lecture tour after his return to New York in late 1909, using seventy photographs that he had taken while on his polar journeys. The tour was orchestrated by theatrical manager William A. Brady. This was not Henson's first experience on the stage. Sixteen years earlier he had toured with Peary in a series of dramatized lectures about their polar adventures. These spectacles included Henson onstage with dogs and were preceded by Henson's traveling through the streets to the lecture clad in Arctic furs.[44] Now that the expeditions were over, Peary was particularly angry that Henson had kept from him some of Henson's own photographs and further that Henson was using the images in public lectures.

In Middletown, Connecticut, on October 16, 1909, Henson dodged (presumably from shyness) the drum corps preparing to meet him at the station. There he delivered two lectures, the first introduced by the mayor and the second, in the evening, by Governor Frank B. Weeks. Henson was "bombarded by questions" and "heartily applauded many times for his quick wit and frank answers."[45] For another of these lectures, at Wonderland Park near Boston, Henson used slides, furs, and sledges as props.[46] Other lectures were less successful due to Henson's inexperience as a speaker, exhaustion, the racist hostility of some audiences, and poor ticket sales. Henson earned about $2,700 from this entire venture.[47] The *Chicago Defender,* a newspaper of the African-American community, gave his performance on February 7 a mixed review, noting that "Mr. Henson is not an orator or scholar, neither is his delivery good, but his discourse was listened to with much interest and pleasure."[48] The tour did not attract sufficient audiences and was aborted in Chicago after a handful of public events.

In 1910 Henson wrote an article titled "A Negro at the North Pole" for the monthly magazine *Worlds Work* and was interviewed for "Matt Henson Tells the Real Story of Peary's Trip," published by the *Boston American* on July 17. Here Henson was frankly critical of his treatment by Peary: "From the moment I declared to Commander Peary that I believed we stood upon the Pole, he apparently ceased to be my friend." It was during these three post-expedition years that Henson prepared his autobiography. The book met with a mixed and modest reception (much as his public lectures had). Allen

Counter speculates that it was neither aimed at, nor read by, a white audience, but it was known quite widely in the black community.[49] Seeing no rise in fortune from the book's publication, Henson took a job briefly as a parking lot attendant in Harlem.

According to Robinson, local politician Charlie Anderson, arranged in 1913 for President William Howard Taft to issue an executive order to provide a government job for Henson in the US Customs House in New York City. Henson served initially as messenger and later as clerk until his retirement at age seventy on a pension of approximately $1,000 a year. In another version of the story, recounted by MacMillan in private correspondence, Marie Peary Stafford believed that her father had arranged for this appointment.[50] In a different alternative explanation, Donald MacMillan credited the appointment to the Peary Arctic Club.[51] However it came about, the pay was meager. Henson's second wife Lucy Jane Ross, whom he married in 1906 (or 1908), worked in a bank during most of their married life, providing the funds to sustain the pair in modest respectability. After Henson's final return in 1909, the pair lived simply in Harlem. They took up residence in the Dunbar Apartments at 246 West 150th Street, #3F, New York City, from 1929 until his death. A plaque dedicated to Henson marks the location.

Because his pension was small, Henson needed money as he entered retirement at age seventy. In 1929 New York representative Fiorello La Guardia introduced a bill to grant retirement to Henson immediately, with benefits, from his civil service job with the Customs House, but the bill did not pass. In 1933 New York representative Joseph A. Gavagan tried again to introduce a bill that would recognize Henson and allow him to retire, but it, too, died.[52] In 1936 Mr. Mitchell, representative from Illinois, introduced a bill to provide a medal for Henson and a pension of $2,500 a year. Again, the effort failed.

Still, Henson enjoyed several public honors in his later years. Many of these were initially from the African-American community and its institutions. In 1909 he was the honoree at a celebration at the Harlem Tuxedo Club—attended by Booker T. Washington, among other dignitaries—where he was presented with a gold watch. Morgan State College conferred an honorary master of science degree in 1924, and there is evidence that Henson lectured at other African-American institutions in that year.[53] The Henson Gletscher/Glacier in North Greenland was named in his honor. In 1929 he received a silver cup from the Bronx Chamber of Commerce on the twentieth anniversary of the Peary party's final celebrated dash to the North Pole, an award that particularly pleased him.[54] Howard University awarded him an honorary degree in 1939.

The pace of honors quickened in the 1940s and came from an increasingly wide range of institutions and organizations. It may not be coincidental that this period, roughly around World War II, saw the emergence of a number of African-

American public figures into national prominence, including Jesse Owens, Paul Robeson, Marian Anderson, Adam Clayton Powell, Ralph Bunche, and the famed Tuskegee Airmen. Beginning in 1940, the city of Phoenix constructed the Matthew Henson Homes designed for African Americans, a project that grew in size and prospered over a sixty-year period. In 1942 a mural project depicting African-American heroes, including Henson, who had contributed to the nation was undertaken for the lobby of the Recorder of Deeds Building in Washington, DC. In 1944 the US Congress gave Henson a duplicate of the silver medal previously awarded to Peary. In 1945 he was awarded a medal by the US Navy.

In 1948 Henson's status in The Explorers Club, originally awarded in 1937, was upgraded to Honorary Membership. Sometime in this period, Henson was interviewed for a television program, although it is unclear that the program was ever aired. In 1948 Henson was the subject of a radio dramatization written by Richard Durham for his series *Destination: Freedom*. This is probably the work, largely derived from *Dark Companion*, that was distributed by the Armed Forced Radio and Television Service during the mid-1950s.[55] And finally in 1948 Donald MacMillan, who was part of the team on the 1909 pole trek, awarded Henson a gold medal from the Chicago Geographical Society. There was some communication among officials of Bowdoin College about an honorary degree, but that proposal, backed by Donald MacMillan, did not come to fruition.[56]

In these years and in the decades following, Henson was the subject of considerable attention from a Baltimore science teacher and newspaperman of African descent, Herbert M. Frisby, who began a campaign to honor Henson that continued after the latter's death. Many of the honors that came to Henson shortly before his death in 1955 or in the years immediately afterward came about through Frisby's efforts. It is clear from Frisby's activities, including travel in polar regions, that this master of public relations relished his self-appointed role as Henson's advocate.

In 1949 Henson received a citation from the US Department of Defense for his contribution to the discovery of the North Pole. In the same year Frisby dropped a steel canister from an airplane over the North Pole that contained Henson-related memorabilia, including US and Maryland flags,[57] a photograph of Henson, a bronze memorial plaque, and perhaps even the Bible that Henson had with him on the northward trek in 1909.

In 1950 Dillard University in New Orleans named its gymnasium Henson Hall. In the same year Henson met President Harry S. Truman. Three years later, Henson was presented by the NAACP with a bronze bust by artist John LaFarge during a ceremony at the Wendell Wilkie Memorial Building in New York City. In 1954 he visited the White House, with his wife, at the invitation of President Dwight David Eisenhower; he was awarded an official citation. In that same year Henson was interviewed for the *One Tenth of a Nation* series from

All American Newsreel. Additionally, he received a lacquered steel medal commemorating the discovery of the pole by the Colored Commercial Association of Chicago.

Matthew Henson died in New York City on March 9, 1955, at the age of eighty-eight, and was buried in Woodlawn Cemetery in the Bronx. More than 1,000 people attended the funeral.[58] His body and that of his wife were disinterred in 1988 and moved to Arlington National Cemetery to be reburied adjacent to the grave of Robert E. Peary.[59]

The life story that emerges from the combination of the autobiography and Robinson's *Dark Companion* indicates in considerable detail what Henson *did,* but it is deficient in indicating what he *thought.* It is especially lacking in ruminations about the heart of the story, Henson's experience in the Far North. Robinson[60] tries to fill in the blanks, depending upon both his imagination and Henson's assistance, but his biography was written many years after Henson's return from the Arctic. Times had changed and memories had faded.

Although sometimes described as Henson's good friend, Robinson, according to the blurb, met Henson only one year before *Dark Companion* was published. Robinson was the son of a member of The Explorers Club, an organization that had elected Henson to membership in 1937. The thoughts Robinson ascribes to Henson, including a kind of puzzlement and resentment about racial attitudes in the United States, seem naive for a man whose extraordinary skill and adaptability had taken him around the world to experience a wide range of cultural diversity. Henson's judgments, as described by Robinson, sound more like the conjectures of a sympathetic, socially progressive biographer from the majority culture of the 1940s than those of an aged, thoughtful African-American man born in the nineteenth century. One must keep in mind that Henson lived through a complex political period when African-American fortunes waxed and waned, from the great hopes of the 1870s through Jim Crow, through the period of prewar northern migration, and finally to the postwar time of tentative recognition for African Americans. That Robinson's book should seem so time-bound and class-based is not surprising for a work whose blurb contends frankly that the author, Bradley Robinson, has "a fine ability to interpret personalities important in our country's history in the light of today's values." To make the story contemporary to the 1940s was an important objective of the author, possibly more important than creating a record of Henson's memories.

After studying both Henson's autobiography and *Dark Companion*, readers are still left with many questions about Henson's true nature. What did Henson make of his travels as cabin boy to China, Japan, North Africa, Russia, and elsewhere? Was he really descended from Josiah Henson, thought to be the model for Uncle Tom in Harriet Beecher Stowe's classic, and if so what did he make of this historical link? What did he really learn from the reputedly kindly Captain Childs, who taught him to read and write? How did Henson react to the cultural differences between the behavior of Eskimos and that of the Peary party toward him? Did he know people in the vigorous intellectual movements centered in the Harlem of his day? Who was George Gardiner,[61] Henson's friend and elder by a few years, whom he came to know when he worked at the American Museum of Natural History in 1897, with whom he lived after returning to New York City in 1902,[62] and in whose apartment he met his future wife in about 1905?[63] What was the subject of their long talks?[64] Was Henson meaningfully involved in a Harlem church while alive, or was his funeral service at the Abyssinian Baptist Church, with Adam Clayton Powell attending, only a social rite? Were the financial difficulties Henson faced when coming back to the United States due entirely to racial discrimination, or was his situation comparable with that of others who returned from this and other polar exploration parties, many of whom died in modest and even dire financial circumstances? Insofar as he was "recognized" by the wider culture in his very last years, was Henson critical of the motivations behind that recognition? Did he feel "used" when recognition finally came? Most puzzling of all, why did Henson accompany Peary for twenty-three years for almost no pay, backbreaking toil, and little recognition? Was it simply because he had "always wanted adventure"?[65]

Readers know from the formulaic and frequent retelling of his life's story what Henson *represented* to his society, but rarely do they get a glimpse of who he actually *was,* especially since he was by nature an adaptor and accommodator. He did not record his thoughts for posterity, either directly or through intermediaries. Because of the paucity and slipperiness of evidence, it is doubtful that a fully satisfactory biography of this elusive man of action can ever be written.

WHO GOT TO THE POLE FIRST?

The usual claimants to first at the North Pole are Robert E. Peary and Frederick A. Cook. Peary announced from Labrador on September 6, 1909, that he had reached the pole on April 6, 1909, in the company of Matthew Henson and four Eskimo guides. Here the chronology gets murky. On September 1, 1909, just before Peary's announcement, Cook proclaimed that it was he who deserved the "prize" of public recognition for this feat, having reached the Pole on April 21, 1908, a full year before Peary's party. On the final lap of his journey, Cook had been accompanied by two Eskimo companions who were later called upon to testify to his feat. Cook's own announcement had been delayed due to the difficulties and travel in and communication from the Far North.

Curiously, neither could present the kind of evidence that scientists expected. Peary's diary for the last days of his journey showed some blank pages and some additional pages, possibly inserted later, on different paper. The diary lacked the specificity that reports of official travel in polar regions usually contained in this and earlier periods. Cook's documentation, part of which was lost, was also insufficient by the standards of science. Neither had persons with them in the final stage of their attempts who had advanced navigation skills and could corroborate their stories. And since there was no landmass at the North Pole, only drifting ice, neither could leave a permanent marker to be checked later by objective observers.

Some have blamed Henson for failing to elucidate this and other controversial Peary claims beyond his usually general statements of support. Thomas D. Davies points out that both Peary critics Dennis Rawlins and Wally Herbert absolve Henson of conspiring in Peary's misstatements.[66] One should keep in mind that however significant Henson's participation in Peary's ventures and claims, it was Peary who was the official decision maker and spokesperson for all expeditions the two embarked upon together.

A river of ink has been spilled over this controversy. Because hard evidence is scant, the arguments usually focus on the moral character of the leaders and the likelihood, based on general behavior and tendencies, that either or both might have faked claims of success. The reported journeys have been analyzed to a minute degree and even, to some extent, replicated.[67]

Ice condition and weather vary, of course, so true replication isn't really possible. In terms of probability, based on reported speeds of travel and amounts of supplies taken and consumed, Peary seems to many people to be the more likely candidate for success, assuming that a choice must be between one and the other. The case is complicated by the fact that the family and descendants of both Cook and Peary steadfastly continue to protect the reputations of their "family heroes" through selective release and interpretation of papers and other means and continue actively to foster the claims of their respective ancestors to this day.

Betraying some exasperation with the competition, Donald MacMillan, who participated in Peary's final push in 1909, wrote in private correspondence to Bradley Robinson, "You know as well as I do that the North Pole has never been discovered and never will be. It is so small that the best microscope in the world cannot locate it."[68] In a letter of June 1962 to John Allen, MacMillan expressed his impatience with the word *discoverer* in these terms: "Man can reach [the North Pole], attain it, but not discover it. Peary was honest in telling me that he hoped that he was within five miles of it! Scott and Amundsen varied in their estimate by 20 miles!" The North Pole is in fact a highly elusive "spot" defined generally as the place where the northern rotational axis intersects the earth's surface. While MacMillan admired Henson for his work for Peary, he was very critical of Henson's lack of gratitude toward the expedition leader in later years and particularly of Henson's agreeing to be designated by his supporters as "co-discoverer of the North Pole."[69]

What interests us here is Henson's role in this debate. It was, in fact, pivotal. As for Peary's claim, Henson was the only member of the team from the United States who accompanied Peary on the final polar quest and the only one with a claim to any ability in scientific navigational skills in the Western sense. But did he, specifically, understand the sextant? MacMillan, generally friendly to Henson but disapproving of his later claims, said no. In private correspondence to Archie Shamblin of the *Santa Ana Register,* he wrote flatly, "Matthew Henson could not take an observation and would not know whether he was at the North Pole or not."[70] Henson, in his very later years, said he could, and therefore he was able to verify Peary's recorded readings. He claimed that he had learned some navigation as a seaman, and that Ross Marvin, on the final Peary expedition, taught him the mathematical part of the required skills.[71] There is some suspicion that Henson might have misunderstood what this claim meant, or that he was encouraged through time to bolster his claim to meet the desires of the press and others that he be considered a full-fledged "explorer" in contrast with an "explorer's assistant." At any rate, Henson's reportage of Peary's rate of progress toward the Pole has convinced many analysts. As supporter of Peary's claim, Henson played a distinctly positive role.

Henson's usually unwavering support of Peary was tainted in later years by Henson's claim, stated first in his autobiography of 1912 and enlarged upon in Robinson's biographical novel of 1947, that it was actually he, Henson, who first set foot upon the spot designated as the North Pole. Neither Peary nor Robert Bartlett, who was the last North American to leave the northward party during the final staged push to the pole, supported this claim. Peary, Henson explained, arrived some time later than he, delayed perhaps by as much as forty-five minutes. If in fact it happened this way—which assumes that the party knew to the snowflake exactly where the Pole was—did it matter? It was clearly Peary's expedition, after all. This is just the sort of detail that could matter to the press, looking for a vivid personality or telling detail on which to hang a story.

Henson was, curiously, involved in Cook's claim to primacy at the pole as well as Peary's. Here the role he played was negative. He had known Cook when the latter served as physician on Peary's voyage to Greenland in 1891–1892. There seems to have been no personal animosity between the two. In Henson's autobiographical work of 1912, however, Henson disparaged Cook's abilities in the hard physical work of polar travel, thus casting doubt on Cook's claim. Henson played another role in the debate when he was called upon to interpret for an interview between Cook's Eskimo companions and MacMillan on the subject of Cook's description of his "discovery" of the Pole. The Eskimos' account, according to Henson, included the statement that they never lost sight of land, thus reinforcing the case against Cook. Suspicions about Cook's veracity concerning both his earlier Mount McKinley and polar claims were taken seriously and probably the reasons that The Explorers Club expelled Cook, a founding member, from its rolls in December 1909.

Partisans for each of the parties seize on many complexities of the case to keep the controversy going with seemingly endless speculation and debate. Supporters of one or the other explorer have included not only individuals and families, but also institutions including the Peary Arctic Club, the National Geographic Society, and even the Congress of the United States. Emotions on the question still run high, and nowhere higher than on the many Internet sites devoted to Henson's role in the controversy.

Beyond the debate on whether Peary or Cook headed the "conquering" party, there is the intriguing question of whether Eskimos[72] might have gotten to the North Pole much earlier, entirely on their own. It is clear that Eskimos had the ability to do so, since it was Eskimo skills that made it possible for Peary and Cook to mount their attempts at all. Would it "count" if the Eskimos got to the magic polar spot first but were unaware of the significance to Western society of that peculiar piece of geography? More to the point, why would the Eskimos, an eminently practical people, have bothered going to an area beyond the land where sustenance, as they knew it, was almost nonexistent? There was probably some oral tradition among Eskimos connected to the farthest northern locale, but the evidence is understandably difficult to identify.

In conversations among historians on this point, one sometimes hears the speculation that Eskimos called this mythic place the "big nail." In fact this term is the title of

Theon Wright's book on the Peary–Cook controversy.[73] This name, Big Nail, may have arisen from a mistranslation of the Eskimo term for "empty place." While the Eskimos were frequently described by polar travelers as having intense curiosity in many areas of life, and especially in technologies applicable to their situation, they were not commonly described as obsessed with the need to explore for its own sake, quite apart from the search for sustenance. Moreover it is virtually unheard of, in the accounts of outsiders, for Eskimos to put themselves and their companions in danger merely to find out what is beyond the next berg. If the Eskimos didn't get there first, it is likely due more to lack of compelling reasons to do so than lack of ability.

Whether Matthew Henson was the first person, or the first non-indigenous person, or the first person of African ancestry, to reach the North Pole should not be the determining factor in the public's interest in his experience or its admiration for his achievements. The designation of "first to the North Pole" would be a simple and handy way to refer to his significance, even if true, but that term would hardly do justice to his life, his place in Arctic history, and his contribution to the literature of exploration as represented by his autobiographical text.

This curiously vitriolic controversy over primacy at the North Pole has obscured the fact that both Peary and Cook respectively made significant contributions to technology and medicine during their polar travels. But the emphasis on who got there first continues to fascinate some readers and to inspire modern publishers appealing to push the envelope in creating titles that emphasize the concept of primacy.

HENSON'S POSTHUMOUS REPUTATION

It was mainly after Henson's death that the broader American public celebrated his role in Arctic exploration. This posthumous wave of recognition is most obvious in the stream of books that has appeared from the 1960s to the current day, the vast majority intended for young-adult and juvenile audiences. These are adulatory works, emphasizing Henson's claims to being "first" in various categories. In order to make Henson's story as exciting as possible for young readers, authors of this adventure genre readily employ action words such as *victorious, conquering, subduing,* and *winning* when describing the achievement.

Juvenile literature, of course, must simplify a story for its readers, and lack of nuance is understandable in that genre. Despite that constraint, some of Henson's biographers have attempted to introduce some subtlety about Henson's importance, emphasizing his responsible role and not his presumed primacy as the first man to set foot on the pole, the first African American to reach the North Pole, or the first in various combinations of these categories. Other authors and publishers seem to have responded to the black pride movement of the past few decades and have emphasized Henson's "blackness" in their titles and narratives. In some of these latter works, Henson is variously described as a black scientist, or geographer, as well as explorer.

It is understandable and entirely appropriate that modern writers and publishers presenting Henson material would want to inspire young people of African-American background by stressing Henson's importance in attaining an objective of the dominant culture, that is, reaching the North Pole, but it is a distortion of the record to suggest that his contributions to the Peary expeditions were widely celebrated by a grateful and respectful nation during his lifetime. The flood of recognition seems, rather, to have coincided with the civil rights movement of the 1960s and decades following. Publishers were quick to see the opportunity for addressing a growing interest in black history, and the result was a spate of publications. Books on Henson were among these.

While Matthew Henson could reasonably be called a hero for what he achieved in exploration, especially given the circumstances of his birth and life, he was in essence part of a team. His role as valued team member has been underemphasized. Henson was, by most accounts, a modest, popular, quiet, and reliable man who was exceptionally skilled in all practical aspects of cold-region exploration. His helpfulness was well known at the time by those closest to him. In fact his Eskimo name, Miy Paluk, means "the kind one." It might be most accurate to say of Henson, as members of The Explorers Club were said to believe, that he "made the discovery possible,"[74] an honorable role in itself.

The forms of published tributes to Henson, issued as multiples, have included freestanding biographies at various reading levels, periodical articles, chapters in school texts and collective histories of famous black persons, and, latterly, encyclopedic listings of outstanding Americans. Others include comic-book-type histories, a super-size coloring book,[75] and posters. Additionally there exist celebratory, mostly small-scale examples of ephemera and collectibles. These include an "activity set" with plastic figurines, a puzzle, a medal, a postcard, trade cards, two series of commemorative dessert plates bearing Henson's image, photographic reproductions, a US postage stamp bearing images of Peary and Henson (1986), and various statuary in plaster, resin, and plastic. Henson has inspired many drawings, paintings, and sculptures.[76]

In addition to the issuing of books and collectibles based on Henson, mainly intended for private consumption, Henson's supporters have also caused him to be celebrated on a large scale in a highly public manner. These are some of his posthumous public honors:

1955   A Memorial Resolution is passed by the Maryland General Assembly commending Henson's contributions and lamenting his death.

1956   Herbert Frisby drops a box from an airplane over the North Pole that contains Henson-related objects (US and Maryland flags, a photograph of Henson, a bronze memorial plaque, and possibly Henson's Bible from his days as explorer).

1961   A plaque honoring Henson is placed in the Maryland State House in Annapolis.

1963   *Ahdoolo! The Biography of Matthew A. Henson,* by Floyd Miller, is published.

1974   Henson appears as a minor figure in E. L. Doctorow's novel *Ragtime* and in the subsequent movie and musical.

1983   The Smithsonian Institution acquires a painting by William H. Johnson, *Commodore Peary and Henson at the North Pole,* c. 1945, a gift of the Harmon Foundation.

1987   The mayor of Washington, DC, declares June 3, 1987, to be Matthew Henson Day.

1987   Henson's Eskimo descendants, including his son
        Ahnahkaq (or Anaukaq) and his five grandchildren,
        are brought to the United States for a visit with
        American relatives and Henson-related sites by Dr.
        Allen Counter, who issues a new edition of Henson's
        autobiography, an account of his meeting with Hen-
        son's northern family, and a documentary on his
        meeting with Henson's descendants in Greenland.

1988   Henson's body and that of his wife Lucy are moved
        to Arlington Cemetery with the permission of Pres-
        ident Ronald Reagan.

1989   A play titled *Poles Apart* by John E Byrd is staged
        in November by the Paul Robeson Theatre in
        Brooklyn.

1998   The USNS *Henson,* an oceanographic research
        ship, is christened.

1998   The Navy League national President participates
        in a wreath-laying ceremony at Arlington National
        Cemetery on November 21 to honor Henson on the
        tenth anniversary of Henson's re-interment to that
        location; Audrey Mebane, Henson's grandniece,
        attends. On November 19, 1998, USNS *Henson* sails
        out of Baltimore with twelve of Henson's descen-
        dants aboard to visit Arlington National Cemetery,
        in the company of navy representatives, the National

Geographic Society, other Henson family members, and many others.

1999   National Public Radio's Alex Chadwick profiles Matthew Henson as one of the unsung heroes on Peary's last North Pole expedition of 1909 (May 17).

2000   Widget Magic creates the first electronic version, in PDF, of Henson's 1912 autobiography in its original form, sold through Amazon.com.

2000   To honor Henson's memory, the National Geographic Society establishes an annual $10,000 scholarship for a minority person from Washington, DC.

2000   The National Geographic Society posthumously awards Henson the Hubbard Medal for one "who with Robert E. Peary led the 1909 American expedition to the North Pole"; it's accepted by Henson's grandniece Audry Mebane.

2000   The dedication of the Matthew Henson Earth Conservation Center on the shores of the Anacostia River at Buzzard Point, Washington, DC.

ca. 2000   The establishment of the Matthew Henson Greenways near the Suitland Parkway and the Potomac River in Maryland.

2001   Moving-image artist Isaac Julien installs a medita-
        tion on Henson as a three-screen video called *True
        North* at Art Basel Miami Beech.

2001–03 The Peary & Henson Foundation is formed by
        Verne Robinson, son of Henson biographer Bradley
        Robinson, to provide educational materials about
        the "partnership" of these two men and their his-
        torical contributions. Robinson also forms the Mat-
        thew Henson Society.

2003   The Annual Matthew Henson Environmental Law
        Fellowship is established at Seattle University Law
        School.

2002   Lucie Idlout, a Canadian Aboriginal rock singer,
        plays the part of Akatingwah, Henson's Greenlandic
        lover, in the play *Two Words for Snow,* staged in
        Toronto.

2008   *A Big Blue Nail*—a play about Henson by Carlyle
        Brown—is staged during January in Chicago by the
        Victory Gardens Theatre.

undated A bust of Henson is placed in Baltimore's National
        Great Blacks in Wax Museum.

MATTHEW HENSON AND
THE EXPLORERS CLUB

A 1947 photograph of Explorers Club members (see insert), including an aged Henson, tells much of the story. Henson is in the first row, flanked by famous explorers and club members Vilhjalmur Stefansson and Peter Freuchen, both of whom supplied introductory matter to *Dark Companion.* In 1937, when he was in his seventy-first year, Henson was elected Life Member of this community of explorers and their enthusiastic, socially prominent supporters, many of whom did some exploration in their own right. Henson's membership was upgraded to Honorary in 1948 "in recognition of outstanding achievements in the attainment of the North Pole."[77] Ootah, an Eskimo who accompanied Peary and Henson on their polar quest, was elected to membership in the Club as well, but like Henson not until some thirty years after the famous journey. On the Club website today, deceased members Peary, Henson, and Ootah are credited with being the first to "reach the North Pole—or at least come close." The Club's official stance on the issue of primacy, as expressed on its website, is that it has no documentation that will resolve the question.

Henson was well known to many of the members, both the socially prominent enthusiasts and the prominent explorers, from his participation in Peary's northward expeditions for more than two decades. Among the early Club members were business and social leaders; the first presidents were

Adolphus W. Greely (1905–06), Frederick A. Cook (1907–08), Robert E. Peary (1909–11; 1913–16), and Vilhjalmur Stefansson (1919–22; 1937–39); and world-famous polar explorers Sir Ernest Shackleton, Sir George Hubert Wilkins, and Roald Amundsen.

The Explorers Club had its origins in the Peary Arctic Club, which was made up of influential, mostly wealthy, backers of Peary's efforts to reach the North Pole. In 1904 The Explorers Club was officially established. Today it occupies a handsome town house on Manhattan's Upper East Side, oversees a library and archive, and maintains a program of sponsorships and activities for members. Women were admitted to the club as members in 1981.

In Henson's days the Club was distinctly exclusive. While he could meet the test of having participated in exploration, Henson was an exceptional member by virtue of background, race, and economic circumstances. It is not surprising that the decision to invite him came under the presidency of Stefansson, who was well known for his social inclusiveness. The primary reason for the invitation was, of course, Henson's extensive experience in the expeditions to the Far North. It was Stefansson who formally introduced Henson at a Club dinner in 1947 when Henson was honored.

The members were sensitive to Henson's financial difficulties. On February 11, 1949, the board of directors requested that members contribute to a fund to benefit Henson. On their behalf, Secretary W. T. Wilson wrote, "He has not sought help from the Club but from other sources the Board has learned of his needs." Club records include a letter from Henson, dated February 20, thanking them for their gift of $250. Henson received another check for $200 in April 1949, and $649 as an additional contribution. Despite his limited funds, Henson did what he could to support the activities of the Club. The archives indicate that he sent $5 in both 1941 and 1944 to support the collation fund; he made another small contribution in 1946 to the Christmas fund.

Henson is reported to have greatly enjoyed his membership and, in turn, the other Club members enjoyed his company. Just two years before his death, there was a club campaign to send this "fine old man" birthday cards from members. Presumably in gratitude, his wife Lucy, after his death, wrote to the club to announce that she intended to leave part of her insurance to the Club in memory of her husband.

Today The Explorers Club houses a bust of Henson by sculptor John Lafarge that was presented in a ceremony on February 9, 1953, sponsored by the National Association for the Advancement of Colored People. Averell Harriman spoke at the event, describing Henson as a "pioneer" for opportunity, demonstrating "the capacity of the Negro to meet the test of merit in free and open competition."

Mementos of Henson are rare, and the Club is pleased to own some of these.[78] The Club has two pairs of Henson's mittens, one of sealskin leather and another of sealskin fur, made presumably by skilled Eskimo women. One of the leather mittens is inscribed "Matthew A. Henson May 5–1934 To —Explorers Club. . . . Worn by me from Cape Sheridan to it—North Pole April 8, 1909." The club also houses a sledge labeled "North Pole Sledge of Matthew Henson & Robert Peary 1909." Since Henson was the master builder of Peary's unique design, he could well have worked on the construction of this one. Finally, gracing the club's lobby is an action-filled painting of Peary and Henson during the final struggle to the pole. The artist was Tom Lovell, who produced the work for *True Magazine*.[79] The club maintains its Henson archival material with great care and continues to celebrate proudly the legacy of one of its most accomplished and famous members.

> DEIRDRE C. STAM
> Palmer School of Library and Information Science
> Long Island University
> September 2008

FOREWORD

Friends of Arctic exploration and discovery, with whom I have come in contact, and many whom I know only by letter, have been greatly interested in the fact of a colored man being an effective member of a serious Arctic expedition, and going north, not once, but numerous times during a period of over twenty years, in a way that showed that he not only could and did endure all the stress of Arctic conditions and work, but that he evidently found pleasure in the work.

The example and experience of Matthew Henson, who has been a member of each and of all my Arctic expeditions, since '91 (my trip in 1886 was taken before I knew Henson) is only another one of the multiplying illustrations of the fact that race, or color, or bringing-up, or environment, count nothing against a determined heart, if it is backed and aided by intelligence.

Henson proved his fitness by long and thorough apprenticeship, and his participation in the final victory which planted the Stars and Stripes at the North Pole, and won for this country the international prize of nearly four centuries, is a distinct credit and feather in the cap of his race.

As I wired Charles W. Anderson, collector of internal revenue, and chairman of the dinner which was given to Henson in New York, in October, 1909, on the occasion of the presentation to him of a gold watch and chain by his admirers:

"I congratulate you and your race upon Matthew Henson. He has driven home to the world your great adaptability and the fiber of which you are made. He has added to the moral stature of every intelligent man among you. His is the hard-earned reward of tried loyalty, persistence, and endurance. He should be an everlasting example to your young men that these qualities will win whatever object they are directed at. He deserves every attention you can show him. I regret that it is impossible for me to be present at your dinner. My compliments to your assembled guests."

It would be superfluous to enlarge on Henson in this introduction. His work in the north has already spoken for itself and him.

Yet two of the interesting points which present themselves in connection with his work may be noted.

Henson, son of the tropics, has proven through years, his ability to stand tropical, temperate, and the fiercest stress of frigid, climate and exposure, while on the other hand, it is well known that the inhabitants of the highest north, tough and hardy as they are to the rigors of their own climate, succumb very quickly to the vagaries of even a temperate climate. The question presents itself at once: "Is it a difference in physical fiber, or in brain and will power, or is the difference in the climatic conditions themselves?"

Again it is an interesting fact that in the final conquest of the "prize of the centuries," not alone individuals, but *races* were represented. On that bitter brilliant day in April, 1909, when the Stars and Stripes floated at the North Pole, Caucasian, Ethiopian, and Mongolian stood side by side at the apex of the earth, in the harmonious companionship resulting from hard work, exposure, danger, and a common object.

R. E. PEARY.

Washington, Dec., 1911.

INTRODUCTION

One of the first questions which Commander Peary was asked when he returned home from his long, patient, and finally successful struggle to reach the Pole was how it came about that, beside the four Esquimos, Matt Henson, a Negro, was the only man to whom was accorded the honor of accompanying him on the final dash to the goal.

The question was suggested no doubt by the thought that it was but natural that the positions of greatest responsibility and honor on such an expedition would as a matter of course fall to the white men of the party rather than the Negro. To this question, however, Commander Peary replied, in substance:

"Matthew A. Henson, my Negro assistant, has been with me in one capacity or another since my second trip to Nicaragua in 1887. I have taken him on each and all of my expeditions, except the first, and also without exception on each of my farthest sledge trips. This position I have given him primarily because of his adaptability and fitness for the work and secondly on account of his loyalty. He is a better dog driver and can handle a sledge better than any man living, except some of the best Esquimo hunters themselves."

In short, Matthew Henson, next to Commander Peary, held and still holds the place of honor in the history of the expedition that finally located the position of the Pole, because he was the best man for the place. During twenty-three years of faithful service he had made himself indispensable. From the position of a servant he rose to that of companion and assistant in one of the most dangerous and difficult tasks that was ever undertaken by men. In extremity, when both the danger and the difficulty were greatest, the Commander wanted by his side the man upon whose skill and loyalty he could put the most absolute dependence and when that man turned out to be black instead of white, the Commander was not only willing to accept the service but was at the same time generous enough to acknowledge it.

There never seems to have been any doubt in Commander Peary's mind about Henson's part and place in the expedition.

Matt Henson, who was born in Charles County, Maryland, August 8, 1866, began life as a cabin-boy on an ocean steamship, and before he met Commander Peary had already made a voyage to China. He was eighteen year old when he made the acquaintance of Commander Peary which gave him his chance. During the twenty-three years in which he was the companion of the explorer he not only had time and opportunity to perfect himself in his knowledge of the books, but he acquired a good practical knowledge of everything that was a necessary part of the daily life in the ice-bound wilderness of polar exploration. He was at times a blacksmith, a carpenter, and a cook. He was thoroughly acquainted with the life, customs, and language of the Esquimos. He himself built the sledges with which the journey to the Pole was successfully completed. He could not merely drive a dog-team or skin a musk-ox with the skill of a native, but he was something of a navigator as well. In this way Mr. Henson made himself not only the most trusted but the most useful member of the expedition."

I am reminded in this connection that Matthew Henson is not the first colored man who by his fidelity and devotion has made himself the trusty companion of the men who have explored and opened up the western continent. Even in the days when the Negro had a little or no opportunity to show his ability as a leader, he proved himself at least a splendid follower, and there are few great adventures in which the American white man has engaged where he has not been accompanied by a colored man.

Nearly all the early Spanish explorers were accompanied by Negroes. It is said that the first ship built in America was constructed by the slaves of Vasquez de Ayllon, who attempted to establish a Spanish settlement where Jamestown, Virginia, was later founded. Balboa had 30 Negroes with him, and they assisted him in constructing the first ship on the Pacific coast. Three hundred slaves were brought to this country by Cortez, the conqueror of Mexico, and it is said that the town of Santiago del Principe was founded by Negro slaves who later rebelled against their Spanish masters.

Of the story of those earlier Negro explorers we have, aside from the Negro Estevan or "little Steve," who was the guide and leader in the search for the fabulous seven cities, almost nothing more than a passing reference in the accounts which have come down to us. Now, a race which has come up from slavery; which is just now for the first time learning to build for itself homes, churches, school; which is learning for the first time to start banks, organize insurance companies, erect manufacturing plants, establish hospitals; a race which is doing all the fundamental things for the first time; which has, in short, its history before it instead of behind; such a race in such conditions needs for its own encouragement, as well as to justify the hopes of its friends, the records of the members of the race who have been a part of any great and historic achievement.

For this reason, as well as for others; for the sake of my race as well as the truth of history; I am proud and glad to welcome this account of his adventure from a man who has not only honored the race of which he is a member, but has proven again that courage, fidelity, and ability are honored and rewarded under a black skin as well as under a white.

BOOKER T. WASHINGTON

Principal, Tuskegee Normal and Industrial Institute.

A BLACK EXPLORER
AT THE NORTH POLE

CHAPTER 1

THE EARLY YEARS:
SCHOOLBOY, CABIN-BOY, SEAMAN, AND
LIEUTENANT PEARY'S BODY-SERVANT
—FIRST TRIPS TO THE ARCTIC

*W*hen the news of the discovery of the North Pole, by Commander Peary, was sent to the world, a distinguished citizen of New York City, well versed in the affairs of the Peary Arctic Club, made the statement, that he was sure that Matt Henson had been with Commander Peary on the day of the discovery. There were not many people who knew who Henson was, or the reason why the gentleman had made the remark, and, when asked why he was so certain, he explained that, for the best part of the twenty years of Commander Peary's Arctic work, his faithful and often only companion was Matthew Alexander Henson.

To-day there is a more general knowledge of Commander Peary, his work and his success, and a vague understanding of the fact that Commander Peary's sole companion from the realm of civilization, when he stood at the North Pole, was Matthew A. Henson, a Colored Man.

To satisfy the demand of perfectly natural curiosity, I have undertaken to write a brief autobiography, giving particularly an account of my Arctic work.

I was born in Charles County, Maryland, August 8, 1866. The place of my birth was on the Potomac River, about forty-four miles below Washington, D. C. Slavery days were over forever when I was born. Besides, my parents were both free born before me, and in my mother's veins ran some white blood. At an early age, my parents were induced to leave the country and remove to Washington, D. C. My mother died when I was seven years old. I was taken in charge by my uncle, who sent me to school, the "N Street School" in Washington, D. C., which I attended for over six years. After leaving school I went to Baltimore, Md., where I shipped as cabin-boy, on board a vessel bound for China. After my first voyage I became an able-bodied seaman, and for four years followed the sea in that capacity, sailing to China, Japan, Manilla, North Africa, Spain, France, and through the Black Sea to Southern Russia.

It was while I was in Washington, D. C., in 1888, that I first attracted the attention of Commander Peary, who at that time was a civil engineer in the United States Navy, with the rank of lieutenant, and it was with the instinct of my race that I recognized in him the qualities that made me willing to engage myself in his service. I accompanied him as his body-servant to Nicaragua. I was his messenger at the League Island Navy Yard, and from the beginning of his second expedition to the Arctic regions, in 1891, I have been a member of every expedition of his, in the capacity of assistant: a term that covers a multitude of duties, abilities, and responsibilities.

The narrative that follows is a record of the last and successful expedition of the Peary Arctic Club, which had as its attainment the discovery of the North Pole, and is compiled from notes made by me at different times during the course of the expedition. I did endeavor to keep a diary or journal of daily events during my last trip, and did not find it difficult aboard the ship while sailing north, or when in winter-quarters at Cape Sheridan, but I found it impossible to make daily entries while in the field, on account of the constant necessity of concentrating my attention on the real business of the expedition. Entries were made daily of the records of temperature and the estimates of distance traveled; and when solar observations were made the results were always carefully noted. There were opportunities to complete the brief entries on several occasions while out on the ice, notably the six day's enforced delay at the "Big Lead," 84° north, the twelve hours preceding the return of Captain Bartlett at 87° 47' north, and the thirty-three hours at North Pole, while Commander Peary was determining to a certainty his position. During the return from the Pole to Cape Columbia, we were so urged by the knowledge of the supreme necessity of speed that the thought of recording the events of that part of the journey did not occur to me so forcibly as to compel me to pay heed to it, and that story was written aboard the ship while waiting for favorable conditions to sail toward home lands.

It was in June, 1891, that I started on my first trip to the Arctic regions, as a member of what was known as the

"North Greenland Expedition." Mrs. Peary accompanied her husband, and among the members of the expedition were Dr. Frederick A. Cook, of Brooklyn, N.Y., Mr. Langdon Gibson, of Flushing, N. Y., and Mr. Eivind Astrüp, of Christiania, Norway, who had the honor of being the companion of Commander Peary in the first crossing of North Greenland—and of having an Esquimo at Cape York become so fond of him that he named his son for him! It was on this voyage north that Peary's leg was broken.

Mr. John M. Verhoeff, a stalwart young Kentuckian, was also an enthusiastic member of the party. When the expedition was ready to sail home the following summer, he lost his life by falling in a crevasse in a glacier. His body was never recovered. On the first and the last of Peary's expeditions, success was marred by tragedy. On the last expedition, Professor Ross G. Marvin, of Cornell University, lost his life by being drowned in the Arctic Ocean, on his return from his farthest north, a farther north than had ever been made by any other explorers except the members of the last expedition. Both Verhoeff and Marvin were good friends of mine, and I respect and venerate their memories.

Naturally the impressions formed on my first visit to the Land of Ice and Snow were the most lasting, but in the coming years I was to learn more and more that such a life was no picnic, and to realize what primitive life meant. I was to live with a people who, the scientists stated, represented the earliest form of human life, living in what is known as the Stone Age, and I was to revert to that stage of life by leaps and bounds, and to emerge from it by the same sudden means. Many and many a time, for periods covering more than twelve months, I have been to all intents an Esquimo, with Esquimos for companions, speaking their language, dressing in the same kind of clothes, living in the same kind of dens, eating the same food, enjoying their pleasures, and frequently sharing their griefs. I have come to love these people. I know every man, woman, and child in their tribe. They are my friends and they regard me as theirs.

After the first return to civilization, I was to come back to the savage, ice- and rock-bound country seven times more. It was in June, 1893, that I again sailed north on board the *Falcon*, a larger ship than the *Kite*, the one we sailed north in on the previous expedition, and with a much larger equipment, including several burros from Colorado, which were intended for ice-cap work, but which did not make good, making better dog-food instead. Indeed the gods made life a burden for the poor brutes from the very start. Mrs. Peary was again a member of the expedition, as well as another woman, Mrs. Cross, who acted as Mrs. Peary's maid and nurse. It was on this trip that I adopted the orphan Esquimo boy, Kudlooktoo, his mother having died just previous to our arrival at the Red Cliffs. After this boy was washed and scrubbed by me, his long hair cut short, and his greasy, dirty clothes of skins and furs burned, a new suit made of odds and ends collected from different wardrobes on the ship made him a presentable Young American. I was proud of him, and he of me. He learned to speak English and slept underneath my bunk.

This expedition was larger in numbers than the previous one, but the results, owing to the impossible weather conditions, were by no means successful, and the following season all of the expedition returned to the United States except Commander Peary, Hugh J. Lee, and myself. When the expedition returned, there were two who went back who had not come north with us. Miss Marie Ahnighito Peary, aged about ten months, who first saw the light of day at Anniversary Lodge on the 12th of the previous September, was taken by her mother to her kin-folks in the South. Mrs. Peary also took a young Esquimo girl, well known among us as "Miss Bill," along with her, and kept her for nearly a year, when she gladly permitted her to return to Greenland and her own people. Miss Bill is now grown up, and has been married three times and widowed, not by death but by desertion. She is known as a "Holy Terror." I do not know the reason why, but I have my suspicions.

The memory of the winter of 1894 and 1895 and the summer following will never leave me. The events of the journey to 87° 6' in 1906 and the discovery of the North Pole in 1909 are indelibly impressed on my mind, but the recollections of the long race with death across the 450 miles of the ice-cap of North Greenland in 1895, with Commander Peary and Hugh Lee, are still the most vivid.

For weeks and weeks, across the seemingly never-ending wastes of the ice-cap of North Greenland, I marched with

Peary and Lee from Independence Bay and the land beyond back to Anniversary Lodge. We started on April 1, 1895, with three sledges and thirty-seven dogs, with the object of determining to a certainty the northeastern terminus of Greenland. We reached the northern land beyond the ice-cap, but the condition of the country did not allow much exploration, and after killing a few musk-oxen we started on June 1 to make our return. We had one sledge and nine dogs.

We reached Anniversary Lodge on June 25, with one dog.

The Grim Destroyer had been our constant companion, and it was months before I fully recovered from the effects of that struggle. When I left for home and God's Country the following September, on board the good old *Kite*, it was with the strongest resolution to never again! no more! forever! leave my happy home in warmer lands.

Nevertheless, the following summer I was again "Northward Bound," with Commander Peary, to help him secure, and bring to New York, the three big meteorites that he and Lee had discovered during the winter of 1894–1895.

The meteorites known as "The Woman" and "The Dog" were secured with comparative ease, and the work of getting the large seventy-ton meteor, known as "The Tent," into such a position as to insure our securing it the following summer, was done, so it was not strange that the following summer I was again in Greenland but the meteorite was not brought away that season.

It is well known that the chief characteristic of Commander Peary is persistency which, coupled with fortitude, is the secret of his success. The next summer, 1897, he was again at the island after his prize, and he got it this time and brought it safely to New York, where it now reposes in the "American Museum of Natural History." As usual I was a member of the party, and my back still aches when I think of the hard work I did to help load that monster aboard the *Hope.*

It was during this voyage that Commander Peary announced his determination to discover the North Pole, and the following years (from 1898 to 1902) were spent in the Arctic.

In 1900, the American record of Farthest North, held by Lockwood and Brainard, was equaled and exceeded; their cairn visited and their records removed. On April 21, 1902, a new American record of 84° 17' was made by Commander Peary, further progress north being frustrated by a lack of provisions and by a lane of open water, more than a mile wide. This lead or lane of open water I have since become more familiarly acquainted with. We have called it many names, but it is popularly known as the "Big Lead." Going north, meeting it can be depended upon. It is situated just a few miles north of the 84th parallel, and is believed to mark the continental shelf of the land masses in the Northern Hemisphere.

During the four years from 1898 to 1902, which were continuously spent in the regions about North Greenland, we had every experience, except death, that had ever fallen to the lot of the explorers who had preceded us, and more than once we looked death squarely in the face. Besides, we had many experiences that earlier explorers did not meet. In January, 1899, Commander Peary froze his feet so badly that all but one of his toes fell off.

After the return home, in 1902, it was three years before Commander Peary made another attack on the Pole, but during those years he was not resting.

He was preparing to launch his final and "sincerely to be hoped" successful expedition, and in July, 1905, in the newly built ship, *Roosevelt*, we were again "Poleward-bound." The following September, the *Roosevelt* reached Cape Sheridan, latitude 82° 27' north, under her own steam, a record unequaled by any other vessel, sail or steam.

Early the next year, the negotiation of the Arctic Ocean was commenced, not as oceans usually are negotiated, but as this ocean must be, by men, sledges, and dogs. The field party consisted of twenty-six men, twenty sledges, and one hundred and thirty dogs.

That was an open winter and an early spring, very desirable conditions in some parts of the world, but very undesirable to us on the northern coast of Greenland. The ice-pack began disintegrating much too early that year to suit, but we pushed on, and had it not been for furious storms enforcing delays and losses of many precious days, the Pole would have been reached. As it was, Commander Peary and his party got to 87° 6' north, thereby breaking *all records*, and in spite of incredible hardships, hunger and cold, returned safely with all of the expedition, and on Christmas Eve the *Roosevelt*, after a most trying voyage, entered New York harbor, somewhat battered but still seaworthy.

Despite the fact that it was to be his last attempt, Commander Peary no sooner reached home than he announced his intention to return, this time to be the last, and this time to win.

However, a year intervened, and it was not until July 6, 1908, with the God-Speed and good wishes of President Roosevelt, that the good ship named in his honor set sail again. The narrative of that voyage, and the story of the discovery of the North Pole, follow.

The ages of the wild, misgiving mystery of the North Pole are over, to-day, and forever it stands under the folds of Old Glory.

Chapter 2

Off for the Pole
—How the Other Explorer's Looked—The
Lamb–Like Esquimos—Arrival at Etah

*J*uly 6, 1908: We're off! For a year and a half I have waited for this order, and now we have cast off. The shouting and the tumult ceases, the din of whistles, bells, and throats dies out, and once again the long, slow surge of the ocean hits the good ship that we have embarked in. It was at one-thirty P. M. to-day that I saw the last hawse-line cast adrift, and felt the throb of the engines of our own ship. Chief Wardwell is on the job, and from now on it is due north.

Oyster Bay, Long Island Sound: We are expecting President Roosevelt. The ship has been named in his honor and has already made one voyage toward the North Pole, farther north than any ship has ever made.

July 7: At anchor, the soft wooded hills of Long Island give me a curious impression. I am waiting for the command to attack the savage ice- and rock-bound fortress of the North, and here instead we are at anchor in the neighborhood of sheep grazing in green fields.

Sydney, N. S., July 17, 1908: All of the expedition are aboard and those going home have gone. Mrs. Peary and the children, Mr. Borup's father, and Mr. Harry Whitney, and some other guests were the last to leave the *Roosevelt*, and have given us a last good-by from the tug, which came alongside to take them off.

Good-by all. Every one is sending back a word to some one he has left behind, but I have said my good-bys a long time ago, and as I waved my hand in parting salutation to the little group on the deck of the tug, my thoughts were with my wife, and I hoped when she next heard of me it would be with feelings of joy and happiness, and that she would be glad she had permitted me to leave her for an absence that might never end.

The tenderfeet, as the Commander calls them, are the Doctor, Professor MacMillan, and young Mr. Borup. The Doctor is a fine-looking, big fellow, John W. Goodsell, and has a swarthy complexion and straight hair; on meeting me he told me that he was well acquainted with me by reputation, and hoped to know me more intimately.

Professor Donald B. MacMillan is a professor in a college in Massachusetts, near Worcester, and I am going to cultivate his acquaintance.

Mr. George Borup is the kid, only twenty-one years old but well set up for his age, always ready to laugh, and has thick, curly hair. I understand he is a record-breaker in athletics. He will need his athletic ability on this trip. I am making no judgments or comments on these fellows now. Wait; I have seen too many enthusiastic starters, and I am sorry to say some of them did not finish well.

All of the rest of the members of the expedition are the same as were on the first trip of the *Roosevelt*:—Commander Peary, Captain Bartlett, Professor Marvin, Chief Engineer Wardwell, Charley Percy the steward, and myself. The crew has been selected by Captain Bartlett, and are mostly strangers to me.

Commander Peary is too well known for me to describe him at length; thick reddish hair turning gray; heavy, bushy eyebrows shading his "sharpshooter's eyes" of steel gray, and long mustache. His hair grows rapidly and, when on the march, a thick heavy beard quickly appears. He is six feet tall, very graceful, and well built, especially about the chest and shoulders; long arms, and legs slightly bowed. Since losing his toes, he walks with a peculiar slide-like stride. He has a voice clear and loud, and words never fail him.

Captain Bartlett is about my height and weight. He has short, curly, light-brown hair and red cheeks; is slightly round-shouldered, due to the large shoulder-muscles caused by pulling the oars, and is as quick in his actions as a cat. His manner and conduct indicate that he has always been the leader of his crowd from boyhood up, and there is no man on this ship that he would be afraid to tackle. He is a young man (thirty-three years old) for a ship captain, but he knows his job.

Professor Marvin is a quiet, earnest person, and has had plenty of practical experience besides his splendid education. He is rapidly growing bald; his face is rather thin, and his neck is long. He has taken great interest in me and, being a teacher, has tried to teach me. Although I hope to perfect myself in navigation, my knowledge so far consists only of knot and splice seamanship, and I need to master the mathematical end.

The Chief Engineer, Mr. Wardwell, is a fine-looking, ruddy-complexioned giant, with the most honest eyes I have ever looked into. His hair is thinning and is almost pure white, and I should judge him to be about forty-five years old. He has the greatest patience, and I have never seen him lose his temper or get rattled.

Charley Peary is Commander Peary's oldest hand, next to me. He is our steward, and sees to it that we are properly fed while aboard ship, and he certainly does see to it with credit to himself.

From Sydney to Hawks Harbor, where we met the *Erik*, has been uneventful except for the odor of the *Erik*, which is loaded with whale-meat and can be smelled for miles. We passed St. Paul's Island and Cape St. George early in the day and through the Straits of Belle Isle to Hawks Harbor, where there is a whale-factory. From here we leave for Turnavik.

We have been racing with the *Erik* all day, and have beaten her to this place. Captain Bartlett's father owns it, and we loaded a lot of boots and skins, which the Captain's father had ready for us. From here we sail to the Esquimo country of North Greenland, without a stop if possible, as the Commander has no intention of visiting any of the Danish settlements in South Greenland.

Cape York is our next point, and the ship is sailing free. Aside from the excitement of the start, and the honor of receiving the personal visit of the President, and his words of encouragement and cheer, the trip so far has been uneventful; and I have busied myself in putting my cabin in order, and making myself useful in overhauling and stowing provisions in the afterhold.

July 24: Still northward-bound with the sea rolling and washing over the ship; and the *Erik* in the distance seems to be getting her share of the wash. She is loaded heavily with fresh whale-meat, and is purposely keeping in leeward of us to spare us the discomfort of the odor.

July 25 and 26: Busy with my carpenter's kit in the Commander's cabin and elsewhere. There has been heavy rain and seas, and we have dropped the *Erik* completely. The *Roosevelt* is going fine. We can see the Greenland coast plainly and to-day, the 29th, we raised and passed Disco Island. Icebergs on all sides. The light at midnight is almost as bright as early evening twilight in New York on the Fourth of July and the ice-blink of the interior ice-cap is quite plain. We have gone through Baffin's Bay with a rush and raised Duck Island about ten A. M. and passed and dropped it by two P. M.

I was ashore on Duck Island in 1891, on my first voyage north, and I remember distinctly the cairn the party built and the money they deposited in it. I wonder if it is still there? There is little use for money up here, and the place is seldom visited except by men from the whalers, when their ships are locked in by ice.

From here it is two hundred miles due north to Cape York.

August 1: Arrived at Cape York Bay and went ashore with the party to communicate with the Esquimos of whom there were three families. They remembered us and were dancing up and down the shore, and waving to us in welcome, and as soon as the bow of the boat had grazed the little beach, willing hands helped to run her up on shore. These people are hospitable and helpful, and always willing, sometimes too willing. As an example, I will tell how, at a settlement farther north, we were going ashore in one of the whale-boats. Captain Bartlett was forward, astraddle of the bow with the boat-hook in his hands to fend off the blocks of ice, and knew perfectly well where he wanted to land, but the group of excited Esquimos were in his way and though he ordered them back, they continued running about and getting in his way. In a very short while the Captain lost patience and commenced to talk loudly and with excitement; immediately Sipsoo took up his language and parrot-like started to repeat the Captain's exact words: "Get back there, get back—how in ---- do you expect me to make a landing?" And thus does the innocent lamb of the North acquire a civilized tongue.

It is amusing to hear Kudlooktoo in the most charming manner give Charley a cussing that from any one else would cause Charley to break his head open.

For the last week I have been busy, with "Matt! The Commander wants you," "Matt do this," and "Matt do that," and with going ashore and trading for skins, dogs, lines, and other things; and also walrus-hunting. I have been up to my neck in work, and have had small opportunity to keep my diary up to date. We have all put on heavy clothing; not the regular fur clothes for the winter, but our thickest civilized clothing, that we would wear in midwinter in the States. In the middle of the day, if the sun shines, the heat is felt; but if foggy or cloudy, the heavy clothing is comfortable.

All of the Esquimos want to come aboard and stay aboard. Some we want and will take along, but there are others we will not have or take along on a bet, and the pleasant duty of telling them so and putting them ashore falls to me. It is not a pleasant job to disappoint these people, but they would be a burden to us and in our way. Besides, we have left them a plentiful supply of needfuls, and our trading with them has been fair and generous.

The "Crow's-Nest" has been rigged upon the mainmast, and this morning, after breakfast, Mr. Whitney, three Esquimos, and myself started in Mr. Whitney's motor-boat to hunt walrus. The motor gave out very shortly after the start, and the oars had to be used. We were fortunate in getting two walrus, which I shot, and then we returned to the ship for the whale-boat. We left the ship with three more Esquimos in the whale-boat, and got four more walrus.

Sunday, at Kangerdlooksoah; the land of the reindeer,

79

and the one pleasant appearing spot on this coast. Mr. Whitney and his six Esquimos guides have gone hunting for deer, and I have been ashore to trade for dogs and furs, and have gotten twenty-seven dogs, sealskin-lines for lashings, a big bearskin, and some foxskins. I try to get furskins from animals that were killed when in full fur and before they have started to shed, but some of the skins I have traded in are raw, and will have to be dried.

I have had the disagreeable job of putting the undesirable ashore, and it was like handling a lot of sulky school children.

Seegloo, the dog-owner, is invited to bring his pack aboard and is easily persuaded. He will get a Springfield rifle and loading-outfit and also a Winchester, if he will sell, and his is more than willing.

And this is the story of day after day from Cape York to Etah Harbor, which we reached on August 12.

Chapter 3

Finding of Rudolph Franke
—Whitney landed—Trading and Coaling
—Fighting the Icepacks

*A*t Etah we take on the final load of coal from the *Erik* and the other supplies she has for us, and from now on it will be farewell to all the world; we will be alone with our company, and our efforts will be towards the north and our evasive goal.

At Etah, on going ashore, we were met by the most hopelessly dirty, unkempt, filth-littered human being any of us had ever seen, or could ever have imagined; a white man with long matted hair and beard, who could speak very little English and that only between cries, whimperings, and whines, and whose legs were swollen out of all shape from the scurvy. He was Rudolph Franke and had been left here the year before by Dr. F. A. Cook, an old acquaintance of mine, who had been a member of other expeditions of the Commander's.

Franke was in a bad way, and the burden of his wail was, "Take me away from this, I have permission, see, here is Dr. Cook's letter," and he showed a letter from Dr. Cook, authorizing him to leave, if opportunity offered. Dr. Goodsell looked him very and pronounced him unfit to remain in the Arctic any longer than it would take a ship to get him out, and the Commander had him kindly treated, cleaned, medicated, and place aboard the *Erik*. The poor fellow's spirits commenced to rise immediately and there is good chance of his recovery and safe return home.

We learn that Dr. Cook, with two Esquimo boys, is over on the Grant Land side, and in probably desperate circumstances, if he is still alive. The Commander has issued orders in writing to Murphy and Billy Pritchard to be on the lookout for him and give him all the help he may need, and has also instructed the Esquimos to keep careful watch for any traces of him, while on their hunting trips.

There is a cache of Dr. Cook's provisions here, which Franke turned over to the Commander, and Mr. Whitney has agreed to help Murphy and Billy to guard it.

Mr. Harry Whitney is one of the party of men who came here on the *Erik* to hunt in this region, and he has decided to stay here at Etah for the winter and wait for a ship to take him out next summer. The other two members of the hunting-party, Mr. Larned and Mr. Norton, returned on the *Erik*. If Mr. Whitney had asked me my advice, I would not have suggested that he remain, because, although he has a fine equipment, there will not be much sport in his experience, and there will be a great deal of roughness. He will have to become like the Esquimos and they will be practically his only companions. However, Mr. Whitney has had a talk with the Commander in the cabin of the *Roosevelt*, and the Commander has given his consent and best wishes. Mr. Whitney's supplies have been unloaded and some additions from the *Erik* made, and there is no reason to fear for his safety.

August 8, 1908: My forty-second birthday. I have not mentioned it to any one, and there's only one other besides myself who knows that to-day I am twice three times seven years of age. Seventeen years ago to-day Commander Peary, hobbling about on his crutches with his right leg in a sling, insisted on giving me a birthday party. I was twenty-five years old then, and on the threshold of my Arctic experience. Never before in my life had the anniversary of my birth been celebrated, and to have a party given in my honor touched me deeply. Mrs. Peary was a member of the expedition then, and I suppose that it was due to her that the occasion was made a memorable one for me. Last year, I was aboard the *Roosevelt* in the shadow of the "Statue of Liberty" in New York Bay, and was treated to a pleasant surprise by my wife.

Commander Peary gave me explicit instructions to get Nipsangwah and Myah ashore as quick as the Creator would let them, but to be sure that their seven curs were kept aboard; these two huskies having exalted ideas as to their rights and privileges. Egingwah, or Karko as we knew him, and Koodlootinah and his family were to come aboard.

Acting under orders, I obeyed, but it was not a pleasant task. I have known men who needed dogs less to pay a great deal more for one pup than was paid to Nipsangwah for his pack of seven. The dogs are a valuable asset to this people and these two men were dependent on their little teams to a greater extent than on the plates and cups of tin which they received in exchange for them.

August 8-9, 1908: Have been trading with the natives without any trouble; they will give anything I want for anything that I have that they want. "It's a shame to take the money," or, as money is unknown up here and has no value, I should say that I should be ashamed to take such an advantage of them, but if I should stop to consider the freight-rates to this part of the world, no doubt a hatchet or a knife is worth just what it can be traded in for.

The ship has been rapidly littering up until it is now in a most perfect state of dirtiness, and in order to get the supplies from the *Erik*, coal, etc., the movable articles, dogs, Esquimos, etc., will have to be shifted and yours truly is helping.

The dogs have been landed on a small island in the bay, where they are safe and cannot run away, and they can have a glorious time, fighting and getting acquainted with each other. Some of the Esquimos' goods are ashore, some aboard the *Erik*, and the rest forward on the roof of the deck-house, while the *Roosevelt* is getting her coal aboard.

The loading of the meat and coal has been done by the crews of the ships, assisted and *hampered* by some of the Esquimos, and I have been walrus-hunting, and taxidermizing; that is, I have skinned a pair of walrus so that they can be stuffed and mounted. This job has been very carefully, and I think successfully, done and the skins have been towed ashore. The hearts, livers, and kidneys have been brought aboard and the meat is to be loaded to-morrow. Two boat-loads of bones have been rowed over to Dog Island for dog-food.

Coaling and stowing of whale-meat aboard the *Roosevelt* as finished at noon, August 15, and all day Sunday, August 16, all hands were at the job transferring to the *Erik* the boxes of provisions that were to be left at the cache at Etah. Bos'n Murphy and Billy Pritchard, the cabin-boy, are to stay as guard until the return of the *Roosevelt* next summer. A blind storm of wind and snow prevented the *Roosevelt* from starting until about two-thirty P. M., when, with all the dogs a-howling, the whistle tooting, and the crew and members cheering, we steamed out of the Harbor into Smith Sound, and a thick fog which compelled half-speed past Littleton Island and into heavy pack-ice.

Captain Bartlett was navigating the ship and his eagle eye found a lane of open water from Cape Sabine to Bache Peninsula and open water from Ellesmere Land half-way across Buchanan Bay, but this lead closed on him, and the *Roosevelt* had to stop. Late in the evening, the ice started to move and grind alongside of the ship, but did no damage except scaring the Esquimos. Daylight still kept up and we went to sleep with our boots on!

From Etah to Cape Sheridan, which was to be our last point north in the ship, consumed twenty-one days of the hardest kind of work imaginable for a ship; actually fighting for every foot of the way against the almost impassable ice. For another ship it would have been impassable, but the *Roosevelt* was built for this kind of work, and her worth and ability had been proven on the voyage of 1905. The constant jolting, bumping, and jarring against the ice-packs, forwards and backwards, the sudden stops and starts and the frequent storms made work and comfort aboard ship all but impossible.

Had it been possible to be ashore at some point of vantage, to witness the struggles of our little ship against her giant adversaries would have been an impressive sight.

I will not dwell on the trying hours and days of her successful battle, the six days of watching and waiting for a chance to get out of our dangerous predicament in Lincoln Bay, the rounding of the difficult capes en route, or the horrible jams in Lady Franklin Bay. The good ship kept at the fight and won by sheer bulldogged tenacity and pluck. Life aboard her during those twenty-one days was not one sweet song, but we did not suffer unusually, and a great deal of necessary work was done on our equipments. The Esquimo women sewed diligently on the fur clothing we were to wear during the coming winter and I worked on the sledges that were to be used. Provisions were packed in compact shape and every one was busy. Two caches of provisions were made ashore in the event of an overland retreat, and the small boats were fully provisioned as a precaution against the loss of the ship. We did not dwell on the thought of losing it, but we took no chances.

Meeting with continual rebuffs, but persistently forging ahead and gaining deliberately day by day, the *Roosevelt* pushed steadily northward through the ice-encumbered waters of Kane Basin, Kennedy and Robeson Channels, and around the northeast corner of Grant Lane to the shelter of Cape Sheridan, which was reached early in the afternoon of September 5, 1908.

CHAPTER 4

PREPARING FOR WINTER AT CAPE SHERIDAN
—THE ARCTIC LIBRARY

*N*ow that we had reached Cape Sheridan in the ship, every one's spirits seemed to soar. It was still daylight, with the sun above the horizon, and although two parties had been landed for hunting, no one seemed to be in any particular hurry. The weather was cold but calm, and even in the rush of unloading the ship I often heard the hum of songs, and had it not been for the fur-jacketed men who were doing the work, it would not have been difficult for me to imagine myself in a much warmer climate.

Of course! in accordance with my agreement with some other members of this expedition I kept my eye on the Commander, and although it was not usual for him to break forth into song, I frequently heard him humming a popular air, and I knew that for the present all was well with him.

With the ship lightened, by being unloaded, to a large extent, of all of the stores, she did not very appreciably rise, but the Commander and the Captain agreed that she could be safely worked considerably closer to the shore, inside of the tide-crack possibly; and the *Roosevelt* was made fast to the ice-foot of the land, with a very considerable distance between her and open water. Her head was pointed due north, and affairs aboard her assumed regulation routine. The stores ashore were contracted, and work on getting them into shape for building temporary houses was soon under way. The boxes of provisions themselves formed the walls, and the roofing was made from makeshifts such as sails, overturned whale-boats, and rocks; and had the ship got adrift and been lost, the houses on shore would have proved ample and comfortable for housing the expedition.

A ship, and a good one like the *Roosevelt*, is the prime necessity in getting an expedition within striking distance of the Pole, but once here the ship (and no other boat, but the *Roosevelt* could get here) is not indispensable, and accordingly all precautions against her loss were taken.

It is a fact that Arctic expeditions have lost their ships early in the season and in spite of the loss have done successful work. The last Ziegler Polar Expedition of 1903–1905 is an example. In the ship *America* they reached Crown Prince Rudolph Island on the European route, and shortly after landing, in the beginning of the long night, the *American* went adrift, and has never been seen since. It is not difficult to imagine her still drifting in the lonely Arctic Ocean, with not a soul aboard (a modern phantom ship in a sea of eternal ice). A more likely idea is that she has been crushed by the ice, and sunk, and the skeleton of her hulk strewn along the bottom of the sea, full many a fathom deep.

However, the depressing probabilities of the venture we are on are not permitted to worry us. The *Roosevelt* is a

"Homer" and we confidently expect to have her take us back to home and loved ones.

In the meantime, I have a steady job carpentering, also interpreting, barbering, tailoring, dog-training, and chasing Esquimos out of my quarters. The Esquimos have the run of the ship and get everywhere except into the Commander's cabin, which they have been taught to regard as "The Holy of Holies." With the help of a sign which tersely proclaims "No Admittance," painted on a board and nailed over the door, they are without much difficulty restrained from going in.

The Commander's stateroom is a *state* room. He has a piano in there and a photograph of President Roosevelt; and right next door he has a private bath-room with a bath-tub in it. The bath-tub is chock-full of impedimenta of a much solider quality than water, but it is to be cleared out pretty soon, and every morning the Commander is going to have his cold-plunge, if there is enough hot water.

There is a general rule that every member of the expedition, including the sailors, must take a bath at least once a week, and it is wonderful how contagious bathing is. Even the Esquimos catch it, and frequently Charley has to interrupt the upward development of some ambitious native, who has suddenly perceived the need of ablutions, and has started to scrub himself in the water that is intended for cooking purposes. If the husky has not gone too far, the water is not washed, and our stew is all the more savory.

89

On board ship there was quite an extensive library, especially on Arctic and Antarctic topics, but as it was in the Commander's cabin it was not heavily patronized. In my own cabin I had Dickens' "Bleak House," Kipling's "Barrack Room Ballads," and the poems of Thomas Hood; also a copy of the Holy Bible, which had been given to me by a dear old lady in Brooklyn, N. Y. I also had Peary's books, "Northward Over the Great Ice," and his last work "Nearest the Pole." During the long dreary midnights of the Arctic winter, I spend many a pleasant hour with my books. I also took along with me a calendar for the years 1908 and 1909, for in the regions of noonday darkness and midnight daylight, a calendar is absolutely necessary.

But mostly I had rougher things than reading to do.

CHAPTER 5

MAKING PEARY SLEDGES
—HUNTING IN THE ARCTIC NIGHT
—THE EXCITABLE DOGS AND THEIR HABITS

I have been busy making sledges, sledges of a different pattern from those used heretofore, and it is expected that they will answer better than the Esquimo type of open-work sledge, of the earlier expeditions. These sledges have been designed by Commander Peary and I have done the work.

The runners are longer, and are curved upwards at each end, so that they resemble the profile of a canoe, and are expected to rise over the inequalities of the ice much better than the old style. Lashed together with sealskin thongs, about twelve feet long, by two feet wide and seven inches high, the load can be spread along their entire length instead of being piled up, and a more even distribution of the weights is made. The Esquimos, used to their style of sledge, are of the opinion that the new style will prove too much for one man and an ordinary team to handle, but we have given both kinds a fair trial and it looks as if the new type has the old beaten by a good margin.

The hunting is not going along as successfully as is desired. The sun is sinking lower and lower, and the different hunting parties return with poor luck, bringing to the ship nothing in some cases, and in others only a few hares and some fish.

The Commander has told me that it is imperative that fresh meat be secured, and now that I have done all that it is positively necessary for me to do here at the ship, I am to take a couple of the Esquimo boys and try my luck for musk-oxen or reindeer, so to-morrow, early in the morning, it is off on the hunt.

This from my diary: Eight days out and not a shot, not a sight of game, nothing. The night is coming quickly, the long months of darkness, of quiet and cold, that, in spite of my years of experience, I can never get used to; and up here at Sheridan it comes sooner and lasts longer than it does down at Etah and Bowdoin Bay. Only a few days' difference, but it *is* longer, and I do not welcome it. Not a sound, except the report of a glacier, broken off by its weight, and causing a new iceberg to be born. The black darkness of the sky, the stars twinkling above, and hour after hour going by with no sunlight. Every now and then a moon when storms do not come, and always the cold, getting colder and colder, and me out on the hunt for fresh meat. I know it; the same old story, a man's work and a dog's life, and what does it amount to? What good is to be done? I am tired, sick, sore, and discouraged.

The main thing was game, but I had a much livelier time with some members of the Peary Arctic Club's expedition known as "our four-footed friends"—the dogs.

The dogs are ever interesting. They never bark, and often bite, but there is no danger from their bites. To get together a team that has not been tied down the night before is a job. You take a piece of meat, frozen as stiff as a piece of sheet-iron, in one hand, and the harness in the together, you single out the cur you are after, make proper advances, and when he comes sniffling and snuffling and all the time keeping at a safe distance, you drop the sheet-iron on the snow, the brute makes a dive, and you make a flop, you grab the nearest thing grabable—ear, leg, or bunch of hair—and do your best to catch his throat, after which, everything is easy. Slip the harness over the head, push the fore-paws through, and there you are, one dog hooked up and harnessed. After licking the bites and sucking the blood, you tie said dog to a rock and start for the next one. It is only a question of time before you have your team. When you have them, leave them alone; they must now decide who is fit to be the king of the team, and so they fight, they fight and fight; and once they have decided, the king is king. A growl from him, or only a look, is enough, all obey, except the females, and the females have their way, for, true to type, the males never harm the females, and it is always the females who start the trouble.

The dogs when not hitched to the sledges were kept together in teams and tied up, both at the ship and while we were hunting. They were not allowed to roam at large, for past experience with these customers had taught us that nothing in the way of food was safe from the attack of Esquimo dogs.

I have seen tin boxes that had been chewed open by dogs in order to get the contents, tin cans of condensed milk being gnawed like a bone, and skin clothing being chewed up like so much gravy. Dog fights were hourly occurrences, and we lost a great many by the ravages of the mysterious Arctic disease, piblokto, which affects all dog life and frequently human life. Indeed, it looked for a time as if we should lose the whole pack, so rapidly did they die, but constant care and attention permitted us to save most of them, and the fittest survived.

Next to the Esquimos, the dogs are the most interesting subjects in the Arctic regions, and I could tell lots of tales to prove their intelligence and sagacity. These animals, more wolf than dog, have associated themselves with the human beings of this country as have their kin in more congenial places of the earth. Wide head, sharp nose, and pointed ears, thick wiry hair, and, in some of the males, a heavy mane; thick bushy tail, curved up over the back; deep chest and fore legs wide apart; a typical Esquimo dog is the picture of alert attention. They are as intelligent as any dog in civilization, and a thousand times more useful. They earn their own livings and disdain any of the comforts of life. Indeed it seems that when life is made pleasant for them they get sick, lie down and die; and when out on the march, with no food for days, thin, gaunt skeletons of their former selves, they will drag at the traces of the sledges and by their uncomplaining conduct, inspire their human companions to keep on.

Without the Esquimo dog, the story of the North Pole, would remain untold; for human ingenuity has not yet devised any other means to overcome the obstacles of cold, storm, and ice that nature has placed in the way then those that were utilized on this expedition.

Chapter 6

The Peary Plan
—A Rain of Rocks—My Friends
The Esquimos

*T*he story of the winter at Cape Sheridan is a story unique in the experience of Arctic exploration. Usually it is the rule to hibernate as much as possible during the period of darkness, and the party is confined closely to headquarters. The Peary plan is different; and constant activity and travel were insisted on.

There were very few days when all of the members of the expedition were together, after the ship had reached her destination. Hunting parties were immediately sent out, for it was on the big game of the country that the expedition depended for fresh meat. Professor Marvin commenced his scientific work, and his several stations were all remote from headquarters; and all winter long, parties were sledging provisions, equipment, etc., to Cape Columbia, ninety-three miles northwest, in anticipation of the journey to the Pole. Those who remained at headquarters did not find life an idle dream. There was something in the way of work going on all of the time. I was away from the ship on two hunting trips of about ten days each, and while at headquarters, I shaped and built over two dozen sledges, besides doing lots of other work.

Naturally there were frequent storms and intense cold, and in regard to the storms of the Arctic regions of North Greenland and Grant Land, the only word I can use to describe them is "terrible," in the fullest meaning it conveys. The effect of such storms of wind and snow, or rain, is abject physical terror, due to the realization of perfect helplessness. I have seen rocks a hundred and a hundred and fifty pounds in weight picked up by the storm and blown for distances of ninety or a hundred feet to the edge of a precipice, and there of their own momentum go hurtling through space to fall in crashing fragments at the base. Imagine the effect of such a rainfall of death-dealing bowlders on the feelings of a little group of three or four, who have sought the base of the cliff for shelter. I have been there and I have seen one of my Esquimo companions felled by a blow from a rock eighty-four pounds in weight, which struck him fairly between the shoulder-blades, literally knocking the life out of him. I have been there, and believe me, I have been afraid. A hundred-pound box of supplies, taking an aerial joy ride, during the progress of a storm down at Anniversary Lodge in 1894, struck Commander Peary a glancing blow which put him out of commission for over a week. These mighty winds make it possible for the herbivorous animals of this region to exist. They sweep the snow from vast stretches of land, exposing the hay and dried dwarf-willows, that the hare, musk-oxen, and reindeer feed on.

The Esquimo families who came north to Cape Sheridan with us on the *Roosevelt* found life much more ideal than down in their native land. It was a pleasure trip for them, with nothing to worry about, and everything provided. Some of the families lived aboard ship all through the winter, and some in the box-house on shore. They were perforce much cleaner in their personal habits than they were wont to be in their own home country, but never for an instant does the odor or appearance of an Esquimo's habitation suggest the rose or geranium. The aroma of an East Side lunch-room is more like it.

There were thirty-nine Esquimos in the expedition, men, women and children; for the Esquimo travels heavy and takes his women and children with him as a matter of course. The women were as useful as the men, and the small boys did the ship's chores, sledging in fresh water from the lake, etc. They were mostly in families; but there were several young, unmarried men, and the unattached, much-married and divorced Miss "Bill," who domiciled herself aboard the ship and did much good work with her needle. She was my seamstress and the thick fur clothes worn on the trip to the Pole were sewn by her. The Esquimos lived as happily as in their own country and carried on their domestic affairs with almost the same care-free irregularity as usual. The best-natured people on earth, with no bad habits of their own, but a ready ability to assimilate the vices of civilization. Twenty years ago, when I first met them, not one used tobacco or craved it. To-day every member of the tribe has had experience with tobacco, craves it, and will give most everything, except his gun, to get it. Even little toddlers, three and four years old, will eat tobacco and, strange to say, it has no bad effect. They get tobacco from the Danish missionaries and from the sailors on board the whaling, seal, and walrus-ships. Whisky has not yet gotten in its demoralizing work.

It is my conviction that the life of this little tribe is doomed, and that extinction is nearly due. It will be caused partly by themselves, and partly by the misguided endeavors of civilized people. Every year their number diminishes; in 1894, Hugh J. Lee took the census of the tribe, and it numbered two hundred and fifty-three; in 1906, Professor Marvin found them to have dwindled to two hundred and seven. At this writing I dare say their number is still further reduced, for the latest news I have had from the Whale Sound region informs me that quite a number of deaths have occurred, and the birth-rate is not high. It is sad to think of the fate of my friends who live in what was once a land of plenty, but which is, through the greed of the commercial hunter, becoming a land of frigid desolation. The seals are practically gone, and the walrus are being quickly exterminated. The reindeer and the musk-oxen are going the same way, for the Esquimos themselves now hunt inland, when, up to twenty years ago, their hunting was confined to the coast and the life-giving sea.

They are very human in their attributes, and in spite of the fact that their diet is practically meat only, their tempers are gentle and mild, and there is a great deal of affection among them. Except between husband and wife, they seldom quarrel; and never hold spite or animosity. Children are a valuable asset, are much loved, never scolded or punished, and are not spoiled. An Esquimo mother washes her baby the same way a cat washes her kittens. There are lots of personal habits the description of which might scatter the reading circle, so I will desist with the bald statement, that, for them, dirt and filth have no terrors.

CHAPTER 7

SLEDGING TO CAPE COLUMBIA
—HOT SOLDERING IN COLD WEATHER

*I*f you get out your geography and turn to the map of the Western Hemisphere you will be able to follow me. Take the seventieth meridian west. It is the major meridian of the Western Hemisphere, its northern land extremity being Cape Columbia, Grant Land; southward it crosses our own Cape Cod and the island of Santo Domingo and runs down through the Andes to Cape Horn, the southern extremity of South America.

The seventieth meridian was our pathway to the Pole, based on the west longitude of 70°. Both Professor Marvin and Captain Bartlett took their observations at their respective farthests, and at the Pole, where all meridians meet, Commander Peary took his elevations of the sun, based on the local time of the Columbian meridian.

Cape Columbia was discovered over fifty years ago, by the intrepid Captain Hall, who gave his life to Arctic exploration, and lies buried on the Greenland coast. From the time of the arrival of the *Roosevelt* at Cape Sheridan, the previous September, communications with Cape Columbia were opened up, the trail was made and kept open all through the winter by constant travel between the ship and the cape.

Loads of supplies, in anticipation of the start for the Pole, were sledged there.

The route to Cape Columbia is through a region of somber magnificence. Huge beetling cliffs overlook the pathway; dark savage headlands, around which we had to travel, project out into the ice-covered waters of the ocean, and vast stretches of wind-swept plains meet the eye in alternate changes. From Cape Sheridan to Cape Columbia is a distance of ninety-three miles. In ordinary weather, it took about three and a half marches, although on the return from the Pole it was covered in two marches, men and dogs breezing in.

On February 18, 1909, I left the *Roosevelt* on what might be a returnless journey. The time to strike had come. Captain Bartlett and Dr. Goodsell had already started. The Commander gave me strict orders to the effect that I must get to Porter Bay, pick up the cache of alcohol left there late in the previous week, solder up the leaks, and take it to Cape Columbia, there to await his arrival. The cause of the alcohol-leakage was due to the jolting of the sledges over the rough ice, puncturing the thin tin of the alcohol-cases.

I wish you could have seen me soldering those tins, under the conditions of darkness, intense cold, and insufficient furnace arrangement I had to endure. If there ever was a job for a demon in Hades, that was it. I vividly recall it. At the same instant I was in imminent danger of freezing to death and being burned alive; and the mental picture of those three fur-clad men, huddled around the little oil-stove heating the soldering-iron, and the hot solder dripping on the tin, is amusing now; but we were anything but amused then. The following is transcribed from my diary:

February 18, 1909: Weather clear, temperature 28° at five A. M. We were ready to leave the ship at seven-thirty A. M., but a blinding gale delayed our start until nine A. M. Two parties have left for Columbia: Professor MacMillan, three boys, four sledges, and twenty-four dogs; and my party of three boys and the same outfit. Each sledge is loaded with about two hundred and fifty pounds or provisions, consisting of pemmican, biscuits, tea, and alcohol. The Arctic night still holds sway, but to-day at noon, far to the south, a thin band of twilight shows, giving promise of the return of the sun, and every day now will increase in light. Heavy going to Porter Bay, where we are to spend the night, and as soon as rested start to work soldering up the thirty-six leaky alcohol tins left there by George Borup last week. Professor MacMillan and his party have not shown up yet. They dropped behind at Cape Richardson and we are keeping a watch for them. Snow still drifting and the wind howling like old times. Have had our evening meal of travel-rations; pemmican, biscuits, and tea and condensed milk, which was eaten with a relish. Two meals a day now, and big work between meals. No sign of Professor MacMillan and his crew, so we are going to turn in. The other igloo is waiting for him and the storm keeps up.

February 19, 1909: It was six A. M. when I routed out the boys for breakfast. I am writing while the tea is brewing. Had a good night sleep last night when I did get to sleep. Snoring, talk about snoring! Sleeping with Esquimos on either side, who have already fallen asleep, is impossible. The only way to get asleep is to wake them up, get them good and wide-awake, inquire solicitously as to their comfort, and before they can get to sleep fall asleep yourself. After that, their rhythmic snores will only tend to soothe and rest you.

Worked all day soldering the tins of alcohol, and a very trying job it was. I converted the oil-stove into an alcohol-burner, and used it to heat the irons. It took some time for me to gauge properly the height above the blue flame of the alcohol at which I would get the best results in heating the irons, but at last we found it. A cradle-shaped support made from biscuit-can wire was hung over the flame about an inch above it, and while the boys heated the irons, I squatted on my knees with a case of alcohol across my lap and got to work. I had watched Mr. Wardwell aboard the ship soldering up the cases and I found that watching a man work, and doing the same thing yourself, were two different matters. I tried to work with mittens on; I tried to work with them off. As soon as my bare fingers would touch the cold metal of the tins, they would freeze, and if I attempted to use the mittens they would singe and burn, and it was impossible to hold the solder with my bearskin gloves on. But keeping everlastingly at it brings success, and with the help of the boys the work was slowly but surely done.

Early this evening Professor MacMillan and his caravan arrived. He complimented me on the success of my work and informed me that they camped at Cape Richardson last night and that the trail had been pretty well blown over by the storm, but that the sledge-tracks were still to be seen. Dead tired, but not cold or uncomfortable. The stew is ready and so am I. Good night!

February 20: Wind died down, sky clear, and weather cold as usual. Our next point is Sail Harbor and after breakfast we set out. The Professor has asked me the most advisable way; whether to keep to the sea-ice or go overland, and we have agreed to follow the northern route, overland across Fielden Peninsula, using Peary's Path. By this route we estimate a saving of eight miles of going, and we will hit the beach at James Ross Bay.

Five P. M.: Sail Harbor. Stopped writing to eat breakfast, and then we loaded up and started. Reached there about an hour ago and from the fresh tracks in the snow, the Captain's or the Doctor's party have just recently left. It was evidently Doctor Goodsell and his crew who were here last; for Captain Bartlett left the *Roosevelt* on February 15 and the Doctor did not leave until the 16th. The going has been heavy, due to loose snow and heavy winds. Also intense cold; the thermometers are all out of commission, due to bubbles; but a frozen bottle of brandy proves that we had at least 45° of cold. The igloo I built last December 5 is the one my party are camped in. Professor MacMillan and his party kept up with us all day, and it was pleasant to have his society. Writing is difficult, the kettle is boiled, so here ends to-day's entry.

February 21: Easy wind, clear sky, but awful cold. Going across Clements Markham Inlet was fine, and we were able to steal a ride on the sledges most of the way, but we all had our faces frosted, and my short flat nose, which does not readily succumb to the cold, suffered as much as did MacMillan's. Even these men or iron, the Esquimos, suffered from the cold, Ootah freezing the great toe of his right foot. Perforce, he was compelled to thaw it out in the usual way; that is, taking off his kamik and placing his freezing foot under my bearskin shirt, the heat of my body thawing out the frozen member.

Cape Colan was reached about half past nine this morning. There we reloaded, and I fear overloaded, the sledges, from the cache which has been placed there. Our loads average about 550 pounds per sledge and we have left a lot of provisions behind.

We are at Cape Good Point, having been unable to make Cape Columbia, and have had to build an igloo. With our overloaded sledges this has been a hard day's work. The dogs pulled, and we pushed, and frequently lifted the heavily loaded sledges through the deep, soft snow; but we did not dump any of our loads. Although the boys wanted to, I would not stand for it. The bad example of seeing some piles of provision-cases which had been unloaded by the preceding parties was what put the idea in their heads.

We will make Cape Columbia to-morrow and will have to do no back-tracking. We are moving forward. I have started for a place, and do not intend to run back to get a better start.

Febrary 22, 1909: Cape Columbia. We left Cafe Good Point at seven A. M. and reached Cape Columbia at eight P. M. No wind, but weather thick and hazy, and the same old cold. About two miles from Good Point, we passed the Doctor's igloo. About a mile beyond this, we passed the "Crystal Palace" that had been occupied by the Captain. Six miles farther north, we passed a second igloo, which had been built by the Doctor's party. How did we know who had built and occupied these igloos? It was easy, as an Esquimo knows and recognizes another Esquimo's handwork, the same as you recognize the handwriting of your friends. I noted the neat, orderly, ship-shape condition of the Captain's igloo, and the empty cocoa-tins scattered around the Doctor's igloo. The Doctor was the only one who had cocoa as an article of supply.

Following the trail four miles farther north, we passed the Captain's second igloo. He had unloaded his three sledges here and gone on to Parr Bay to hunt musk-oxen. We caught up with the Doctor and his party at the end of the ice-foot and pushed on to Cape Columbia. We found but one igloo here and I did the "after you my dear Alphonse," and the Doctor got the igloo. My boys and I have built a good big one in less than an hour, and we are now snug and warm.

CHAPTER 8

In Camp at Columbia
—Literary Igloos—The Magnificent
desolation of the Arctic

Our heavy furs had been made by the Esquimo women on board the ship and had been thoroughly aired and carefully packed on the sledges. We were to discard our old clothes before leaving the land and endeavor to be in the cleanest condition possible while contending with the ice, for we knew that we would get dirty enough without having the discomfort of vermin added. It is easy to become vermin-infested, and when all forms of life but man and dog seem to have disappeared, the bedbug still remains. Each person had taken a good hot bath with plenty of soap and water before we left the ship, and we had given each other what we called a "prize-fighter's hair-cut." We ran the clippers from forehead back, all over the head, and we looked like a precious bunch but we had hair enough on our heads by the time we came back from our three months' journey, and we needed a few more baths and new clothes.

When I met Dr. Goodsell at Cape Columbia, about a week after he had left the ship, he had already raised quite a beard, and, as his hair was black and heavy, it made quite a change in his appearance. The effect of the long period of darkness had been to give his complexion a greenish-yellow tinge. My complexion reminded him of a ginger cake with too much saleratus in it.

February 23: Heavy snow-fall but practically no wind this morning at seven o'clock, when Dr. Goodsell left his igloo for Cape Colan to pick up the load he had left there when he lightened his sledges, also some loads of pemmican and biscuits that had been cached. We had supper together and also breakfast this morning, and as we ate we laughed and talked, and I taught him a few tricks for keeping himself warm.

In spite of the snow, which was still falling, I routed out my boys, and in the dark we left camp for the western side of the cape, to get the four sledge-loads of rations that had been taken there the previous November. Got the loads and pushed south to Cape Aldrich, which is a point on the promontory of Cape Columbia. From Cape Aldrich the Commander intends to attack the sea-ice.

After unloading the supplies on the point, we came back to camp at Cape Columbia. Shortly afterwards Captain Bartlett came into camp from his musk-ox-hunt around Parr Bay. He had not shot a thing and was very tired and discouraged, but I think he was glad to see me. He was so hungry that I gave him all the stew, which he swallowed whole.

MacMillan and his party showed up about an hour after the Captain, and very shortly after George Borup came driving in, like "Ann Eliza Johnson, a swingin' down the line." I helped Mr. Borup build his igloo, for which he was grateful.

He is a plucky young fellow and is always cheerful. He told us that Professor Marvin, according to the schedule, had left the ship on the 20th, and the Commander on the 21st, so they must be well on the way.

While waiting in this camp for the Commander and Professor Marvin to arrive, we had plenty of work; re-adjusting the sledge-loads and also building snow-houses and banking them with blocks of snow, for the wind had eroded one end of my igloo and completely razed it to the level of the ground, and a more solidly constructed igloo was necessary to withstand the fury of the gale.

We kept a fire going in one igloo and dried our mittens and kamiks. Though the tumpa, tumpa, plunk of the banjo was not heard, and our camp-fires were not scenes of revelry and joy, I frequently did the double-shuffle and an Old Virginia break-down, to keep my blood circulating.

The hours preceding our advance from Cape Columbia were pleasantly spent, though we lost no time in literary debates. There were a few books along.

Out on the ice of the Polar ocean, as far as reading matter went, I think Dr. Goodsell had a very small set of Shakespeare, and I know that I had a Holy Bible. The others who went out on the ice may have had reading matter with them, but they did not read it out loud, and so I am not in a position to say what their literary tastes were.

Even on shipboard, we had no pigskin library or five-foot shelf of sleep-producers, but each member had some favorite books in his cabin, and they helped to form a circulating library.

While we waited here, we had time to appreciate the magnificent desolation about us. Even on the march, with loaded sledges and tugging dogs to engage attention, unconsciously one finds oneself with wits wool-gathering and eyes taking in the scene, and suddenly being brought back to the business of the hour by the fiend-like conduct of his team.

There is an irresistible fascination about the regions of northernmost Grant Land that is impossible for me to describe. Having no poetry in my soul, and being somewhat hardened by years of experience in that inhospitable country, words proper to give you an idea of its unique beauty do not come to mind. Imagine gorgeous bleakness, beautiful blankness. It never seems broad, bright day, even in the middle of June, and the sky has the different effects of the varying hours of morning and evening twilight from the first to the last peep of day. Early in February, at noon, a thin band of light appears far to the southward, heralding the approach of the sun, and daily the twilight lengthens, until early in March, the sun, a flaming disk of fiery crimson, shows his distorted image above the horizon. This distorted shape is due to the mirage caused by the cold, just as heat-waves above the rails on a railroad-track distort the shape of objects beyond.

The south sides of the lofty peaks have for days reflected the glory of the coming sun, and it does not require an artist to enjoy the unexampled splendor of the view. The snows covering the peaks show all of the colors, variations, and tones of the artist's palette, and more. Artists have gone with us into the Arctic and I have heard them rave over the wonderful beauties of the scene, and I have seen them at work trying to reproduce some of it, with good results but with nothing like the effect of the original. As Mr. Stokes said, "it is color run riot."

To the northward, all is dark and the brighter stars of the heavens are still visible, but growing fainter daily with the strengthening of the sunlight.

When the sun finally gets above the horizon and swings his daily circle, the color effects grow less and less, but then the sky and cloud-effects improve and the shadows in the mountains and clefts of the ice show forth their beauty, cold blues and grays; the bare patches of the land, rich browns; and the whiteness of the snow is dazzling. At midday, the optical impression given by one's shadow is of about nine o'clock in the morning, this due to the altitude of the sun, always giving us long shadows. Above us the sky is blue and bright, bluer than the sky of the Mediterranean, and the clouds from the silky cirrus mare's-tails to the fantastic and heavy cumulus are always objects of beauty. This is the description of fine weather.

Almost any spot would have been a fine one to get a round of views from; at Cape Sheridan, our headquarters, we were bounded by a series of land marks that have become historical; to the north, Cape Hecla, the point of departure of the 1906 expedition; to the west, Cape Joseph Henry, and beyond, the twin peaks of Cape Columbia rear their giant summits out to the ocean.

From Cape Columbia the expedition was now to leave the land and sledge over the ice-covered ocean four hundred and thirteen miles north—to the Pole!

CHAPTER 9

READY FOR THE DASH TO THE POLE
—THE COMMANDER'S ARRIVAL

*T*he Diary—February 23: Heavy snowfall and furious winds; accordingly intense darkness and much
discomfort.

There was a heavy gale blowing at seven o'clock in the
morning, on February 22, and the snow was so thick and drifty
that we kept close to our igloos and made no attempt to do
more than feed the dogs. My igloo was completely covered with
snow and the one occupied by Dr. Goodsell was blown away, so
that he had to have another one, which I helped to build.

The wind subsided considerably, leaving a thick haze, but
after breakfast, Professor MacMillan, Mr. Borup, and their
parties, left camp for Cape Colan, to get the supplies they had
dumped there, and carry them to Cape Aldrich. I took one
Esquimo, Pooadloonah, and one sledge from the Captain's
party, and with my own three boys, Ooblooyah, Ootah, and
I-forget-his-name, and a howling mob of dogs, we left for the
western side of Cape Columbia, and got the rest of the pemmican and biscuits. On the way back, we met the Captain,
who was out taking exercise. He had nothing to say; he did not
shake hands, but there was something in his manner to show
that he was glad to see us. With the coming of the daylight a

man gets more cheerful, but it was still twilight when we left Cape Columbia, and melancholy would sometimes grip, as it often did during the darkness of midwinter.

Captain Bartlett helped us to push the loaded sledges to Cape Aldrich and nothing was left at Cape Columbia.

When we got back to camp we found Professor Marvin and his party of three Esquimos there. They had just reached the camp and were at work building an igloo.

Professor Marvin came over to our igloo and changed his clothes; that is, in a temperature of at least 45° below zero, by the light of my lantern he coolly and calmly stripped to the pelt, and proceeded to cloth himself in the new suit of reindeerskin and polar bearskin clothing, that had been made for him by the Esquimo woman, Ahlikahsingwah, aboard the *Roosevelt*. It had taken him and his party five days to make the trip from Sheridan to Columbia.

February 26: This from my log: "Clear, no wind, temperature 57° below zero." Listen! I will tell you about it. At seven A. M. we quit trying to sleep and started the pot a-boiling. A pint of hot tea gave us a different point of view, and Professor Marvin handed me the thermometer, which I took outside and got the reading; 57° below; that is cold enough. I have seen it lower, but after forty below the difference is not appreciable.

I climbed to the highest pinnacle of the cape and in the gathering daylight gazed out over the ice-covered ocean to get an idea of its condition. At my back lay the land of sadness, just below me the little village of snow-houses, the northernmost city on the earth (Commander Peary give it the name Crane City), and, stretching wide and far to the northward, the irresistible influence that beckoned us on; broken ice, a sinister chaos, through which we would have to work our way. Dark and heavy clouds along the horizon gave indication of open water, and it was easy to see that the rough and heavy shore-ice would make no jokes for us to appreciate.

About an hour or so after the midday meal, a loud outcry from the dogs made me go outside to see what was up. This was on the afternoon of February 26. I quickly saw what the dogs were excited about.

With a "Whoop halloo," three Komaticks were racing and tearing down the gradient of the land to our camp, and all of us were out to see the finish. Kudlooktoo and Arkeo an even distance apart; and, heads up, tails up, a full five sledge-lengths ahead, with snowdust spinning free, the dog-team of the ever victorious Peary in the lead. The caravan came to a halt with a grandstand finish that it would have done you good to witness.

The Commander didn't want to stop. He immediately commenced to shout and issue orders, and, by the time he had calmed down, both Captain Bartlett and George Borup had loaded up and pushed forward on to the ice of the Arctic Ocean, bound for the trophy of over four hundred years of effort. The Peary discipline is the iron hand ungloved. From now on we must be indifferent to comfort, and like poor little Joe, in "Bleak House" we must always be moving on.

CHAPTER 10

FORWARD! MARCH!

Commander Peary was an officer of the United States Navy, but there never was the slightest military aspect to any of his expeditions. No banners flying, no trumpets blaring, and no sharp, incisive commands. Long ago, crossing the ice-cap of North Greenland, he carried a wand of bamboo, on one end of which was attached a little silk guidon, with a star embroidered on it, but even that had been discarded and the only thing military about this expedition was his peremptory "Forward! March! What flags we had were folded and stowed on Commander Peary's sledge, and broken-out only at the North Pole.

Captain Bartlett and Mr. George Borup were all alert and at attention, the command of preparation and the command of execution were quickly given in rapid succession, and they were off.

From the diary.

February 28, 1909: A bright, clear morning. Captain Bartlett and his crew, Ooqueah, Pooadloonah, and Harrigan; and George Borup and Karko, Seegloo, and Keshungwah, have set sail and are on their way.

Captain Bartlett made the trail and George Borup was the scout, and a rare "Old Scout" he was. He kept up the going for three days and then came back to the land to start again with new loads of supplies.

The party that stayed at Crane City until March 1, consisted of Commander Peary, MacMillan, Goodsell, Marvin, myself, and fourteen Esquimos, whom you don't know, and ninety-eight dogs, that you may have heard about.

The dogs were double-fed and we put a good meal inside ourselves before turning-in on the night of February 28, 1909. The next morning was to be our launching, and we went to sleep full of the thought of what was before us. From now on it was keep on going, and keep on—and we kept on; sometimes in the face of storms of wind and snow that it is impossible for you to imagine.

Day does not break in the Arctic regions, it just comes on quietly the same as down here, but I must say that at daybreak on March 1, 1909, we were all excitement and attention. A furious wind was blowing, which we took as a good omen; for, on all of Commander Peary's travelings, a good big, heavy, storm of blinding snow has been his stirrup-cup and here he had his last. Systematically we had completed our preparations on the two days previous, so that, by six A. M. of the 1st of March, we were ready and standing at the upstanders of our sledges, awaiting the command "Forward! March!"

Already, difficulties had commenced. Ooblooyah and Slocum (Esquimo name, Inighito, but on account of his dilatory habits, known as Slocum) were incapacitated; Ooblooyah with a swelled knee, and Slocum with a frozen heel. The cold gets you in most any place, up there.

I and my three boys were ordered to take the lead. We did so, at about half past six o'clock in the morning. Forward! March! And we were off.

Chapter 11

Fighting Up the Polar Sea —Held Up by the "Big Lead"

*F*ollowing the trail made by Captain Bartlett, we pushed off, every man at the upstander of his sledge to urge his team by whip and voice. It was only when we had perfect going over sheets of young ice that we were able to steal a ride on the sledges.

The trail led us over the glacial fringe for a quarter of a mile, and the going was fairly easy, but, after leaving the land ice-foot, the trail plunged into ice so rough that we had to use pickaxes to make a pathway. It took only about one mile of such going, and my sledge split.

"Number one," said I to myself, and I came to a halt. The gale was still blowing, but I started to work on the necessary repairs. I have practically built one sledge out of two broken ones, while out on the ice and in weather almost as bad as this; and I have almost daily during the journey had to repair broken sledges, sometimes under fiercer conditions; and so I will describe this one job and hereafter, when writing about repairing a sledge, let it go at that.

Cold and windy. Undo the lashings, unload the load, get out the brace and bit and bore new holes, taking plenty of time, for, in such cold, there is danger of the steel bit breaking.

Then, with gloved hands, thread the sealskin thongs through the hole. The fingers freeze. Stop work, pull the hand through the sleeve, and take your icy fingers to your heart; that is, put your hand under your armpit, and when you feel it burning you know it has thawed out. Then start to work again. By this time the party has advanced beyond you and, as orders are orders, and you have been ordered to take the lead, you have to start, catch up, and pass the column before you have reached your station.

Of course, in catching up and overtaking the party, you have the advantage of the well-marked trail they have made. Once again in the lead; and my boy, Ootah, had to up and break his sledge, and there was some more tall talking when the Commander caught up with us and left us there mending it. A little farther on, and the amiable Kudlooktoo, who was in my party at the time, busted his sledge. You would have thought that Kudlooktoo was the last person in Commander Peary's estimation, when he got through talking to him and telling him what he thought of him. The sledge was so badly broken it had to be abandoned. The load was left on the spot where the accident happened, and Kudlooktoo, much chastened and crestfallen, drove his team of dogs back to the land for a new sledge.

We did not wait for him, but kept on for about two hours longer, when we reached the Captain's first igloo, twelve miles out; a small day's traveling, but we were almost dead-beat, from having battled all day with the wind, which had blown a full-sized gale. No other but a Peary party would have attempted to travel in such weather. Our breath was frozen to our hoods of fur and our cheeks and noses frozen. Spreading our furs upon the snow, we dropped down and endeavored to sleep, but sound sleep was impossible. It was a night of Plutonian Purgatory. All through the night I would wake from the cold and beat my arms or feet to keep the circulation going, and I would hear one or both of my boys doing the same. I did not make any entries in the diary that day, and there was many a day like it after that.

It was cold and dark when we left camp number one on the morning of March 2, at half past six o'clock. Breakfast had warmed up a bit, but the hard pemmican had torn and cut the roofs and sides of our mouths so that we did not eat a full meal, and we decided that at our next camp we would boil the pemmican in the tea and have a combination stew. I will say now that this experiment was tried, but it made such an unwholesome mess that it was never repeated.

The Captain's and Borup's trail was still evident, in spite of the low drifts of the snow, but progress was slow. We were still in the heavy rubble-ice and had to continuously hew our way with pickaxes to make a path for the sledges. While we were at work making a pathway, the dogs would curl up and lie down with their noses in their tails, and we would have to come back and start them, which was always the signal for a fight or two. We worked through the belt of rubble-ice at last, and came up with the heavy old floes and rafters of ice-blocks, larger than very large flag-stones and fully as thick as they were long and wide; the fissures between them full of the drifted snow. Even with our broad snow-shoes on, we sank knee-deep, and the dogs were in up to their breasts, the sledges up to the floors and frequently turning over, so it was a long time before we had covered seven miles, to be stopped by open water. I took no chances on this lead, although afterwards I did not hesitate at more desperate looking leads than this was. Instead of ferrying across on a block of ice, I left one of my boys to attend the dogs and sledges, and with Ootah I started to reconnoiter. We found that there were two leads, and the safest way to cross the first was to go west to a point where the young ice was strong enough to bear the weight of the sledges. We got across and had not gone very far before the other lead, in spite of a detour to the east, effectually blocked us. Starting back to the sledges, Ootah said he was *"damn feel good,"* and in Esquimo gave me to understand that he was going back to the ship. I tried to tell him different, as we walked back; and when we reached camp we found the Commander and his party, who had just come in; and the Commander gave Ootah to distinctly understand that he was not going back just yet. Orders were given to camp, and while the igloos were being built, Marvin and MacMillan took soundings. There had been more daylight than on the day before, and the gale had subsided considerably, but it was dark when we turned in to have our evening meal and sleep.

March 3: Right after breakfast, my party immediately started, taking the trail I had found the day previous. Examining the ice, we went to the westward, until we came to the almost solid new ice, and we took a chance. The ice commenced to rafter under us, but we got across safely with our loads, and started east again, for two miles; when we found ourselves on an island of ice completely surrounded by the heavy raftered ice. Here we halted and mended sledges and in the course of an hour the whole party had caught up. The ice had begun to rafter and the shattering reports made a noise that was almost ear-splitting, but we pushed and pulled and managed to get out of the danger-zone, and kept going northwestward, in the hope of picking up the trail of the Captain and Borup, which we did after a mile of going. Close examination of the trail showed us that Borup and his party had retraced their steps and gone quite a distance west in order to cross the lead. It was on this march that we were to have met Borup and his party returning, so Marvin and his boy Kyutah were sent to look them up. The rest of the party kept on in the newly found trail and came to the igloo and cache that had been left there by Borup. The Commander went into the igloo, and we made the dogs fast and built our own igloos, made our tea and went to sleep.

March 4: Heavy snow fall; but Commander Peary routed out all hands, and by seven o'clock we were following the Captain's trail. Very rough going, and progress slow up to about nine o'clock, when conditions changed. We reached heavy, old floes of waving blue ice, the best traveling on sea ice I had ever encountered in eighteen years' experience. We went so fast that we more than made up for lost time and at two o'clock, myself in the lead, we reached the igloo built by Captain Bartlett. It had been arranged that I should stop for one sleep at every igloo built by the Captain, and that he should leave a note in his igloo for my instructions; but, in spite of these previous arrangements, I felt that with such good traveling it would be just as wise to keep on going, and so we did, but it was only about half or three-quarters of an hour later when we were stopped by a lead, beside which the Captain had camped. With Ootah and Tommy to help, we built an igloo and crawled inside. Two hours later, the Commander and his party arrived, and we crawled out and turned the igloo over to him. Tommy, Ootah, and I then built another igloo, crawled inside, and blocked the doorway up with a slab of snow, determined not to turn out again until we had had a good feed and snooze.

From my diary, the first entry since leaving the land; with a couple of comments added afterward:

March 5: A clear bright morning, 20° below zero; quite comfortable. Reached here yesterday at two-forty-five P. M., after some of the finest going I have ever seen. Commander Peary, Captain Bartlett, and Dr. Goodsell here, and fourteen Esquimos. First view of the sun to-day, for a few minutes at noon, makes us all cheerful. It was a crimson sphere, just balanced on the brink of the world. Had the weather been favorable, we could have seen the sun several days earlier. Every day following he will get higher and higher, until he finally swings around the sky above the horizon for the full twenty-four hours.

Early in the morning of the 5th, Peary sent a detachment of three Esquimos, in charge of MacMillan, back to bring in Borup's cache, left by him at the point where he turned back to return to the land for more loads. This detachment was back in camp by four o'clock in the afternoon of the same day. Nothing left to do but to rearrange the loads and wait for the lead to close.

The land is still in sight. Professor Marvin has gone back with two boys and is expected to keep on to the alcohol cache at Cape Columbia, turn back and meet us here, or, if the ice freezes, to follow us until he catches up with us. We are husbanding our fuel, and two meals a day is our programme. We are still south of the Big Lead of 1906, but to all intents and purposes this is it. I am able to recognize many of the characteristics of it, and I feel sure it is the same old lead that gave us many an anxious hour in our upward and downward journey three years ago.

Fine weather, but we are still south of the 84th parallel and this open water marks it. 8° below zero and all comfortable. We should be going twenty or twenty-five miles a day good traveling, but we are halted by this open water.

March 7: Professor MacMillan came into camp to-day with the cache he had picked up. There was quite a hullabaloo among the boys, and a great deal of argument as to who owned various articles of provender and equipment that had been brought into camp by MacMillan, and even I was on the point of jumping into the fracas in order to see fair play, until a wink from MacMillan told me that it was simply a put-up job of his to disconcert the Esquimos. Confidentially and on the side he has been dressing his heel, which in spite of all keeps on freezing, and is in very bad shape. His kamiks stick to the loose flesh and the skin will not form. All of the frost has been taken out, but I think skin-grafting is the only thing that will cure it. He wants to keep on going and asks me how far we have gone and wants to know if he shall tell Commander Peary about his injury. I have advised him to make a clean breast of it, but he feels good for a week or so more, and it is up to him.

We eat, and sleep, and watch the lead, and wonder. Are we to be repulsed again? Is the unseen, mysterious guardian of this mist-covered region foiling us? The Commander is taking it with a great deal more patience than he usually has with obstacles, but in the face of this one he probably realizes the necessity of a calm, philosophic mood.

Captain Bartlett has been here longer than any of us, and he is commencing to get nervous. Commander Peary and he have done what is nautically known as "swinging the ship," for the purpose of correcting compass errors, and after that there is nothing for them to do but wait. Captain Bartlett describes it as "Hell on Earth"; the Commander has nothing to say, and

I agree with him. Dr. Goodsell reads from his little books, studies Esquimo language, writes in his diary and talks to me and the rest of the party, and waits.

Professor MacMillan, with his eye ever to the south, and an occasional glance at his frozen heel, cracks a joke and bids us be cheerful. He is one *man*, and has surely made good. His first trip to this forsaken region, yet he wakes up from his sleep with a smile on his face and a question as to how a nice, large, juicy steak would go about now. This is no place for jokes, yet his jokes are cheering and make us all feel more light-hearted. He is the "life of the funeral" and by his cheerfulness has kept our spirits from sinking to a dead level, and when the Esquimos commenced to get cranky, by his diplomacy he brought them to think of other subjects than going back to the ship.

He has started to kid us along by instituting a series of competitions in athletic endeavors, and the Esquimos fall for it like the Innocents that they are, and that is the object he is after. They have tried all of their native stunts, wrestling, boxing, thumb-pulling, and elbow tests; and each winner has been awarded a prize. Most of the prizes are back on the ship and include the anchors, rudders, keel and spars. Everything else has long since been given away, and these people have keen memories.

The Big Lead has no attraction for the Esquimos and the waiting for a chance to cross it has given them much opportunity to complain of cold feet. It is fierce, listening to their whines and howls. Of all yellow-livered curs deliver me. We have the best Esquimos in the tribe with us, and expect them to remain steadfast and loyal, but after they have had time to realize their position, the precariousness of it begins to magnify and they start in to whimper, and beg to be allowed to go back. They remember the other side of this damnable open water and what it meant to get back in 1906. I do not blame them, but I have had the Devil's own time in making my boys and some of the others see it the way the Commander wants us to look at it.

Indeed, two of the older ones, Panikpah and Pooadloonah, became so fractious that the Commander sent them back, with a written order to Gushue on the ship, to let them pack up their things and take their families and dogs back to Esquimo land, which they did. When the *Roosevelt* reached Etah the following August, on her return, these two men were there, fat and healthy, and merrily greeted us. No hard feelings whatever.

March 10: We could have crossed to-day, but there was a chance Marvin and Borup catching up with their loads of alcohol, etc. Whether they catch up or not, to-morrow, early, we start across, and the indications are that the going will be heavy, for the ice is piled in rafters of pressure-ridges.

It was exasperating; seven precious days of fine weather lost; and fine weather is the exception, not the rule, in the Arctic. Here we were resting in camp, although we were not extremely tired and nowhere near exhausted. We were ready and anxious to travel on the 5th, next morning after we reached the "Big Lead," but were perforce compelled to inaction. And so did we wait for nearly seven days beside that lead, before conditions were favorable for a crossing.

But early in the morning of March 11th the full party started; through the heaviest of going imaginable. Neither Borup nor Marvin had caught up, but we felt that unless something had happened to them, they would surely catch up in a few more days.

CHAPTER 12

PIONEERING THE WAY
—BREAKING SLEDGES

*M*arch 11, 1990: Clear, 45°. Off we go! Marvin and Borup have not yet shown up, but the lead is shut and the orders since yesterday afternoon have been to stand by for only twelve hours more; and while the tea is brewing I am using the warmth to write. We could have crossed thirty hours ago, but Commander Peary would not permit us to take chances; he wants to keep the party together as long as possible, and expects to have to send at least eight men back after the next march. MacMillan is not fit, and there are four or five of the natives who should be sent away. Three Esquimos apiece are too many, and I think Commander Peary is about ready to split the different crews of men and dogs. He himself is in very good shape and, due to his example, Captain Bartlett has again taken the field. A heavy storm of wind and snow is in progress, but the motion of the ice remains satisfactory.

This is not a regular camp. We are sheltered north of a huge paleocrystic floeberg; and the dogs are at rest, with their noses in their tails. Dr. Goodsell has set his boys to work building an igloo, which will not be needed, for I see Ooqueah and Egingwah piling up the loads on their sledges, and Professor MacMillan is very busy with his own personal sledge.

No halt, only a breathing spell and, as I have predicted, we are on our way again. This is an extremely dangerous zone to halt or hazard in. The ice is liable to open here at any moment and let us either sink in the cold, black water or drift on a block of frozen ice, much too thin to enable us to get on to the heavy ice again. Three miles wide at least.

The foregoing was written while out on the ice of the Arctic Ocean, just after crossing the raftered hummocks of the ice of the Big Lead. While we were waiting for the rest of the expedition to gather in, I slumped down behind a peak of land or paleocrystic ice, and made the entry in my diary. We were not tired out; we had had more than six days' rest at the lead; and when it closed we pushed on across the pressure-ridges on to the heavy and cumbrous ice of the circumpolar sea. We were sure that we had passed the main obstruction, and in spite of the failure of Marvin and Borup to come in with the essentials of fuel-alcohol and food, Commander Peary insisted on pushing forward.

Prof. Donald B. MacMillan was with the party, but Commander Peary knew, without his telling him, that he was really no longer fit to travel, and Dr. Goodsell was not as far north of the land as original plans intended, so when both MacMillan and Goodsell were told that they must start back to the ship, I was not surprised.

It was March 14 that the first supporting-party finally turned back. It was my impression that Professor MacMillan would command it, but Commander Peary sent the Doctor back in charge, with the two boys Arco and Wesharkoupsi. A few hours before the turning back of Dr. Goodsell, an Esquimo courier from Professor Marvin's detachment had overtaken us, with the welcome news that both Borup and Marvin, with complete loads, were immediately in our rear, safe across the lead that had so long delayed us. I was given instructions to govern my conduct for the following five marches and I was told to be ready to start right after breakfast.

Dr. Goodsell came to me, congratulated me and, with the best wishes for success, bade me good-by. He was loath to go back, but he returned to the ship with the hearty assurance of every one that he had done good and effective work, equal to the best efforts of the more experienced members of the party.

My boys, Ootah, Ahwatingwah, and Koolootingwah, under my command started north, to pioneer the route for five full marches, and it was with a firm resolve that I determined to cover a big mileage. We had been having extreme cold weather, as low as 59° below zero, and on the morning my party started the thermometers in the camp showed 49° below zero.

An hour's travel brought us to a small lead, which was avoided by making a detour, and about four miles beyond this lead we came up to heavy old floes, on which the snow lay deep and soft. The sledges would sink to the depth of the cross-bars. Traveling was slow, and the dogs became demons; at one time, sullen and stubborn; then wildly excited and savage; and in our handling of them I fear we became fiendlike ourselves. Frequently we would have to lift them bodily from the pits of snow, and snow-filled fissures they had fallen into, and I am now sorry to say that we did not do it gently. The dogs, feeling the additional strain, refused to make the slightest effort when spoken to or touched with the whip, and to break them of this stubbornness, and to prevent further trouble, I took the leader or king dog of one team and, in the presence of the rest of the pack, I clubbed him severely. The dogs realized what was required of them, and that I would exact it of them in spite of what they would do, and they became submissive and pulled willingly, myself and the Esquimos doing our share at the upstanders.

We got over the heavy floe-ice, to find ourselves confronted with jagged, rough ice, where we had to pickax our way. In one place we came to pressure-ridges separated by a deep gulch of very rough and uneven ice, in crossing which it took two men to manage each sledge, and another man to help pull them up on to the more even ice. We crossed several leads, mostly frozen over, and kept on going for over twelve hours. The mileage was small and, instead of elation, I felt discouragement. Two of the sledges had split their entire length and had to be repaired, and the going had been such that we could not cover any distance. We had a good long rest at the Big Lead for over six days, but at the end of this, my first day's pioneering, I was as tired out as I have ever been. It should be understood that while I was pioneering I was carrying the full-loaded sledges with about 550 pounds, while the other parties that were in the lead never carried but half of the regular load, which made our progress much slower.

March 15: Bright, clear, and I am sure as cold as the record-breaking cold of the day previous. We made an early start, with hopes high; but the first two hours' traveling was simply a repetition of the going of the day before. But after that, and to the end of the day's march, the surface of the ice over which we traveled was most remarkably smooth. The fallen snow had packed solid into the areas of rough ice and on the edges of the large floes. The dogs, with tails up and heads out, stamped off mile after mile in rapid succession, and when we camped I conservatively made the estimate fifteen miles. It has to be good going to make such a distance with loaded sledges, but we made it and I was satisfied.

March 16: We started going over ice conditions similar to the good part of the day before, but our hopes were soon shattered when the ice changed completely and, from being stationary, and distinct motion become observable. The movement of the ice increased, and the rumbling and roaring as it raftered, was deafening. A dense fog, the sure indication of open water, overhung us, and in due time we came to the open lead, over which small broken floes were scattered, interspersed with thin young ice. These floes were hardly thick enough to hold a dog safely, but, there being no other way, we were obliged to cross on them. We set out with jaws squared by anxiety. A false step by any one would mean the end. With the utmost care, the sledges were placed on the most solid floes, and, with Ootah, the most experienced, in the lead, we followed in single file. Once started, there was no stopping; but push on with the utmost care and even pressure. You know that we got across, but there were instants during the crossing when I had my strongest doubts. After crossing the lead, the ice condition became horrible. Almost at the same time, three of the sledges broke, one sledge being completely smashed to pieces. We were forced to camp and start to work making two whole sledges from the wreckage of the three broken ones.

We had barely completed this work when the Commander, the Captain, Marvin, Borup, and Esquimos came in. I was glad to see them all again, especially the smiling face of George Borup, whom I had not seen since the day he left Cape Columbia.

We learned that MacMillan had been sent back to the ship on the 15th, that the party had been delayed on the second day's march by a new lead, which widened so rapidly and to such an extent that it was feared to be the twin sister of the Big Lead farther back.

March 17: The whole party, with the exception of Professor Marvin and his detachment, remained in camp. Marvin was sent ahead to plot a route for the next marches of the column, and the party in camp busied itself in the general work of repairing sledges and equipment.

The morning of the 18th found the main column ready to start, and it did, in spite of the dreary outlook due to the condition of the weather and of the ice. Thermometer 40° below zero, and the loose ice to our right and in front distinctly in motion, but fortunately moving to the northward. A heavy wind of the force of a gale was at our backs, and for the first three miles our progress was slow. The hummocks of ice in wild disarrangement, and so difficult to cross that repeatedly the sledges were overturned; and one sledge was broken so badly that a halt had to be made to repair it. While repairing the sledge, our midday lunch of crackers was eaten. The dogs were not fed anything, experience having taught us that dogs will work better with hope for a reward in the future than when it is past.

All that day the air was thick with haze and frost and we felt the cold even more than when the temperature was lower with the air clear. The wind would find the tiniest opening in our clothing and pierce us with the force of driving needles. Our hoods froze to our growing beards and when we halted we had to beak away the ice that had been formed by the congealing of our breaths and from the moisture of perspiration exhaled by our bodies. When we finally camped and built our igloos, it was not with any degree of comfort that we lay down to rest. Actually it was more comfortable to keep on the march, and when we did rest it was fatigue that compelled.

CHAPTER 13

THE SUPPORTING-PARTIES BEGIN TO TURN BACK

*M*arch 19: We left camp in a haze of bitter cold; the ice conditions about the same as the previous day; high rafters, huge and jagged; and we pickaxed the way continuously. By noontime, we found ourselves alongside of a lead covered by a film of young ice. We forced the dogs and they took it on the run, the ice undulating beneath them, the same as it does when little wanton boys play at *tickley benders*, often with serious results, on the newly formed ice on ponds and brooks down in civilization. Our *tickley benders* were not done in the spirit of play, but on account of urgent necessity, and as it was I nearly suffered a serious loss of precious possessions.

One of the sledges, driven by Ahwatingwah, broke through the ice and its load, which consisted of my extra equipment, such as kamiks, mittens, etc., was thoroughly soaked. Luckily for the boy, he was at the side of the sledge and escaped a ducking. Foolishly I rushed over, but, quickly realizing my danger, I slowed down, and with the utmost care he fished out the sledge, and the dogs, shaking as with palsy, were gently urged on. Walking wide, like the polar bear, we crept after, and without further incident reached the opposite side of the lead. My team had reached there before me and, with human intelligence, the dogs had dragged the sledge to a place of safety and were sitting on their haunches, with ears cocked forward, watching us in our precarious predicament. They seemed to rejoice at our deliverance, and as I went among them and untangled their traces I could not forbear giving each one an affectionate pat on the head.

For the next five hours our trail lay over heavy pressure ridges, in some places sixty feet high. We had to make a trail over the mountains of ice and then come back for the sledges. A difficult climb began. Pushing from our very toes, straining every muscle, urging the dogs with voice and whip, we guided the sledges. On several occasions the dogs gave it up, standing still in their tracks and we had to hold the sledges with the strength of our bones and muscles to prevent them from sliding backwards. When we had regained our equilibrium the dogs were again started, and in this way we gained the tops of the pressure-ridge.

Going down on the opposite side was more nerve-racking. On the descent of one ride, in spite of the experienced care of Ootah, the sledge bounded away from him, and at a declivity of thirty feet was completely wrecked. The frightened dogs dashed wildly in every direction to escape the falling sledge, and as quickly as possible we slid down the steep incline, at the same time guiding the dogs attached to the two remaining sledges. We rushed over, my two boys and I, to the spot where the poor dogs stood trembling with fright. We released them from the tangle they were in, and, with kind words and pats of the hand on their heads, quieted them. For over an hour we struggled with the broken pieces of the wreck and finally lashed them together with strips of *oog-sook* (seal-hide). We said nothing to the Commander when he caught up with us, but his quick eye took in at a glance the experience we had been through. The repairs having been completed, we again started. Before us stretched a heavy, old floe, giving us good going until we reached the lead, when the order was given to camp. We built our igloos, and boiled the tea and had what we called supper.

Commander Peary called me over to his igloo and gave me my orders: first; that I should at once select the best dogs of the three teams, as the ones disqualified by me would on the following morning be sent back to the ship, in care of the third supporting party, which was to turn back. Secondly; that I should rearrange the loads on the remainder of the sledges, there now being ten in number. It was eight P. M. when I began work and two the following morning when I had finished.

March 20: During the night, the Commander had a long talk with Borup, and in the morning my good friend, in command of the third supporting party, bade us all good by and took his detachment back to land and headquarters. There were three Esquimos and seventeen dogs in his party. A fine and plucky young man, whose cheerful manner and ready willingness had made him a prime favorite; and he had done his work like an old campaigner.

At the time of Borup's turning southward, Captain Bartlett, with two Esquimos, started out to the north to make trail. He was to act as pioneer. At ten-thirty A. M., I, with two Esquimos, followed; leaving at the igloos the Commander and Professor Marvin, with four Esquimos. The system of our marches from now on was that the first party, or pioneers, which consisted of Captain Bartlett, myself, and our Esquimos, should be trail-making, while the second party, consisting of Commander Peary and Marvin, with their Esquimos, should be sleeping; and while the first party was sleeping, the second should be traveling over the trail previously made. The sun was above the horizon the whole twenty-four hours of the day, and accordingly there was no darkness. Either the first or second party was always traveling, and progress was hourly made.

March 21: Captain Bartlett got away early, leaving me in camp to await the arrival of Commander Peary and Marvin, with their party; and it was eight A. M. when they arrived. Commander Peary instructed me to the effect that, when I overtook the Captain, I should tell him to make as much speed as possible.

The going was, for the first hour, over rough, raftered ice. Great care and caution had to be observed, but after that we reached a stretch of undulated, level ice, extending easily fifteen miles; and the exhilarating effect made our spirits rise. The snow-covering was soft, but with the help of our snowshoes we paced off the miles, and at noon we caught up with the Captain and his boys. Together we traveled on, and at the end of an hour's going we halted for our noon-meal, consisting of a can of tea and three biscuits per man, the dogs doing the hungry looking on, as dogs have done and do and will do forever. As we sat and ate, we joshed each other, and the Esquimo boys joined in the good-natured raillery.

The meal did not detain us long, and soon we were pushing on again as quickly as possible over the level ice, fearing that if we delayed the condition of the ice would change, for changes come suddenly, and frequently without warning. At nine P. M. we camped, the Captain having been on the go for fifteen hours, and I for thirteen; and we estimated that we had a good fourteen miles to our credit.

March 22 was the finest day we had, and it was a day of unusual clearness and calm; practically no wind and a cloudless sky. The fields of ice and snow sparkled and glistened and the daylight lasted for the full twenty-four hours. It was six A. M. when Egingwah, the Commander's Esquimo courier, reached our camp, with the note of command and encouragement; and immediately the Captain and I left camp.

Stretching to the northward was a brilliantly illuminated, level, and slightly drifted snow-plain, our imperial highway, presenting a spectacle grand and sublime; and we were truly grateful and inwardly prayed that this condition would last indefinitely. Without incident or accident, we marched on for fifteen hours, pacing off mile after mile in our steady northing, and at nine P. M. we halted. It was then we realized how utterly fatigued and exhausted we were. It took us over an hour and a half to build our igloos. We had a hard time finding suitable snow conditions for building them, and the weather was frightfully cold. The evening meal of pemmican-stew and tea was prepared, the dogs were fed, and we turned in.

March 23: Our sleep-banked eyes were opened by the excitement caused by the arrival of Marvin and his division. He reported the same good going that we had had the day before, and also that he had taken an elevation of the sun and computed his latitude as 85° 46' north. We turned the igloos over to Marvin and his Esquimos, who were to await the arrival of the Commander, and Captain Bartlett and myself got our parties under way.

Conditions are never similar, no two days are the same; and our going this day was nothing like the paradise of the day before. At a little distance from the igloos we encountered high masses of heavily-rubbled, old ice. The making of a trail through these masses of ice caused us to use our pick-axes continuously. It was backing and filling all of the time. First we would reconnoiter, then we would hew our way and make the trail, then we would go back and, getting in the traces, help the dogs pull the sledges, which were still heavily loaded. This operation was repeated practically all the day of March 23, except for the last hour of traveling, when we zigzagged to the eastward, where the ice appeared less formidable, consisting of small floes with rubble ice between and a heavy, old floe beyond. There we camped. The latitude was 85° 46' north.

The course from the land to the Pole was not direct and due north, for we followed the lines of least resistance, and frequently found ourselves going due east or west, in order to detour around pressure ridges, floebergs, and leads.

March 24: Commander Peary reached camp shortly after six A. M., and after a few brief instructions, we started out. The going not as heavy as the day previous; but the sky overcast, and a heavy drift on the surface made it decidedly unpleasant for the dogs. For the first six hours the going was over rough, jagged ice, covered with deep, soft snow; for the rest of the day it improved. We encountered comparatively level ice, with a few hummocks, and in places covered with deep snow. We camped at eight P. M., beside a very heavy pressure-ridge as long as a city street and as high as the houses along the street.

March 25: Turned out at four-thirty A. M., to find a steadily falling snow storm upon us. We breakfasted, and fifteen minutes later we were once more at work making trail. Our burly neighbor, the pressure-ridge, in whose lee we had spent the night, did not make an insuperable obstacle, and in the course of an hour we had made a trail across it, and returned to the igloo for the sledges. We found that the main column had reached camp, and after greetings had been given, Commander Peary called me aside and gave me my orders; to take the trail at once, to speed it up to the best of my ability and cover as much distance as possible; for he intended that I should remain at the igloo the following day to sort out the best dogs and rearrange the loads, as Marvin was to turn back with the fourth supporting-party. My heart stopped palpitating, I breathed easier, and my mind was relieved. It was not my turn yet, I was to continue onward and there only remained one person between me and the Pole—the Captain. We knew Commander Peary's general plan: that, at the end of certain periods, certain parties would turn south to the land and the ship; but we did not know who would comprise or command those parties and, until I had the Commender's word, I feared that I would be the next after Borup. At the same time, I did not see how Marvin could travel much longer, as his feet were very badly frozen.

Obedient to the Commander's orders, the Captain, I, and our Esquimos, left camp with loaded sledges and trudged over the newly made trail, coming to rough ice which stretched for a distance of five miles, and kept us hard at back-straining, shoulder-wrenching work for several hours. The rest of the day's march was over level, unbroken, young ice; and the distance covered was considerable.

March 26: The Commander and party reached the igloo at ten-forty-five A. M. Captain Bartlett had taken to the trail at six A. M., and was now miles to the northward, out of sight. I immediately started to work on the task assigned me by the Commander, assorting the dogs first, so that the different king dogs could fight it out and adjust themselves to new conditions while I was rearranging the loads.

At twelve, noon, Professor Marvin took his final sight, and after figuring it out told me that he made it 86° 38' north.

145

The work of readjusting the loads kept me busy until seven P. M. While doing this work I came across my Bible that I had neglected so long, and that night, before going to sleep, I read the twenty-third Psalm, and the fifth chapter of St. Matthew.

March 27: I was to take the trail at six A. M., but before starting I went over to Marvin's igloo to bid him good-by. In his quiet, earnest manner, he advised me to keep on, and hoped for our success; he congratulated me and we gave each other the strong, fraternal grip of our honored fraternity and we confidently expected to see each other again at the ship. My good, kind friend was never again to see us, or talk with us. It is sad to write this. He went back to his death, drowned in the cold, black water of the Big Lead. In unmarked, unmarbled grave, he sleeps his last, long sleep.

CHAPTER 14

BARTLETT'S FARTHEST NORTH —HIS QUIET GOOD-BY

*L*eaving the Commander and Marvin at the igloos, my party took up the Captain's trail northward. It was expected that Peary would follow in an hour and that at the same time Marvin would start his return march. After a few minutes' going, we came to young ice of this season, broken up and frozen solid, not difficult to negotiate, but requiring constant pulling; leaving this, we came to an open lead which caused us to make a detour to the westward for four miles. We crossed on ice so thin that one of the sledge-runners broke through, and a little beyond one of the dogs fell in so completely that it was a precarious effort to rescue him; but we made it and, doglike, he shook the water out of his fur and a little later, when his fur froze, I gave him a thorough beating; not for falling in the water, but in order to loosen the ice-particles, so that he could shake them off. Poor brute, it was no use, and in a short while he commenced to develop symptoms of the dread piblokto, so in mercy he was killed. One of the Esquimo boys did the killing.

Dangerous as the crossing was, it was the only place possible, and we succeeded far better than we had anticipated. Beyond the lead we came to an old floe and, beyond that, young ice of one season's formation, similar to that which had been encountered earlier in the day. Before us lay a heavy, old floe, covered with soft, deep snow in which we sank continually; but it was only five P. M. when we reached the Captain's igloo. Anticipating the arrival of the Commander, we built another igloo, and about an hour and a half later the Commander and his party came in.

March 28: Exactly 40° below zero when we pushed the sledges up to the curled-up dogs and started them off over rough ice covered with deep soft snow. It was like walking in loose granulated sugar. Indeed I might compare the snow of the Arctic to the granules of sugar, without their saccharine sweetness, but with freezing cold instead; you can not make snowballs of it, for it is too thoroughly congealed, and when it is packed by the wind it is almost as solid as ice. It is from the packed snow that the blocks used to form the igloo-walls are cut.

At the end of four hours, we came to the igloo where the Captain and his boys were sleeping the sleep of utter exhaustion. In order not to interrupt the Captain's rest, we built another igloo and unloaded his sledge, and distributed the greater part of the load among the sledges of the party. The Captain, on awakening, told us that the journey we had completed on that day had been made by him under the most trying conditions, and that it had taken him fourteen hours to do it. We were able to make better time because we had his trail to follow, and, therefore, the necessity of finding the easiest way was avoided. That was the object of the scout or pioneer party and Captain Bartlett had done practically all of it up to the time he turned back at 87° 48' north.

March 29: You have undoubtedly taken into consideration the pangs of hunger and of cold that you know assailed us, going Poleward; but have you ever considered that we were thirsty for water to drink or hungry for fat? To eat snow to quench our thirsts would have been the height of folly, and as well as being thirsty, we were continuously assailed by the pangs of a hunger that called for the fat, good, rich, oily, juicy fat that our systems craved and demanded.

Had we succumbed to the temptations of thirst and eaten the snow, we would not be able to tell the tale of the conquest of the Pole; for the result of eating snow is death. True, the dogs licked up enough moisture to quench their thirsts, but we were not made of such stern stuff as they. Snow would have reduced our temperatures and we would quickly have fallen by the way. We had to wait until camp was made and the fire of alcohol started before we had a chance, and it was with hot tea that we quenched our thirsts. The hunger for fat was not appeased; a dog or two was killed, but his carcass went to the Esquimos and the entrails were fed to the rest of the pack. We ate no dogs on this trip, for various reasons, mainly, that the eating of dog is only a last resort, and we had plenty of food, and raw dog is flavorless and very tough. The killing of a dog is such a horrible matter that I will not describe it, and it is permitted only when all other exigencies have been exhausted. An Esquimo does not permit one drop of blood to escape.

The morning of the 29th of March 1909, a heavy and dense fog of frost spicules overhung the camp. At four A. M., the Captain left camp to make as far a northing as possible. I with my Esquimos followed later. On our way we passed over very rough ice alternating with small floes, young ice of a few months' duration and one old floe. We were now beside a lead of over three hundred feet in width, which we were unable to cross at that time because the ice was running steadily, though to the Northward. Following the trail of the Captain's igloo, the order to camp was given, as going forward was impossible. The whole party was together farther north than had ever been made by any other human beings, and in perfectly good condition; but the time was quickly coming when the little party would have to be made smaller and some part of it sent back. We were too fatigued to argue the question.

We turned in for a rest and sleep, but soon turned out again in pandemonium incomprehensible; the ice moving in all directions, our igloos wrecked, and every instant our very lives in danger. With eyes dazed by sleep, we tried to guide the terror-stricken dogs and push the sledges to safety, but rapidly we saw the party being separated and the black water begin to appear amid the roar of the breaking ice floes.

To the westward of our igloo stood the Captain's igloo, on an island office, which revolved, while swiftly drifting to the eastward. On one occasion the floe happened to strike the main floe. The Captain, intently watching his opportunity, quickly crossed with his Esquimos. He had scarcely set foot on the opposite floe when the floe on which he had been previously isolated swung off, and rapidly disappeared.

Once more the parties were together. Thoroughly exhausted, we turned in and fell asleep, myself and the Esquimos too dumb for utterance, and Commander Peary and Bartlett too full of the realization of our escape to have much to say.

The dogs were in very good condition, taking everything into consideration.

When we woke up it was the morning of another day, March 30, and we found open water all about us. We could not go on until either the lead had frozen or until it had raftered shut. Temperature 35° below zero, and the weather clear and calm with no visible motion of the ice. We spend the day industriously in camp, mending foot-gear, harness, clothing, and looking after the dogs and their traces. This was work enough, especially untangling the traces of the bewildered dogs. The traces, snarled and entangled, besides being frozen to the consistency of wire, gave us the hardest work; and, owing to the activity of the dogs in leaping and bounding over each other, we had the most *unideal* conditions possible to contend with, and we were handicapped by having to use mitted instead of ungloved fingers to untangle the snarls of knots. Unlike Alexander the Great, we dared not cut the "Gordian Knots," but we did get them untangled.

About five o'clock in the afternoon, the temperature had fallen to 43° below zero, and at the same time the ice began to move again. Owing to the attraction of the moon, the mighty flanks of the earth were being drawn by her invisible force, and were commencing again to crack and be rent asunder.

We loaded up hurriedly and all three parties left the camp and crossed over the place where recently had been the open lead, and beyond for more than five miles, until we reached the heavier and solid ice of the large floes. Northward our way led, and we kept on in that direction accordingly, at times crossing young ice so thin that the motion of the sledges would cause the ice to undulate. Over old floes of the blue, hummocky kind, on which the snow had fallen and become packed solid, the rest of this day's journey was completed. We staggered into camp like drunken men, and built our igloos by force of habit rather than with the intelligence of human beings.

It was continuously daylight, but such a light as never was on land or sea.

The next day was April 1, and the Farthest North of Bartlett. I knew at this time that he was to go back, and that I was to continue, so I had no misgivings and neither had he. He was ready and anxious to take the backtrail. His five marches were up and he was glad of it, and he was told that in the morning he must turn back and knit the trail together, so that the main column could return over a beaten path.

Before going to sleep, Peary and he (Captain Bartlett) had figured out the reckoning of the distance, and, to insure the Captain's making at least 88° north, Peary let him have another go, for a short distance northward, and at noon on the day of his return, the observations showed that Captain Bartlett had made 87° 47' North Latitude, or practically 88° north. "Why, Peary," he said, "it is just like every day," and so it was, with this exception, like every day in the Arctic, but with all of every day's chances and hazards. The lion-like month of March had passed. Captain Bartlett bade us all farewell. He turned back from the Farthest North that had ever been reached by any one, to insure the safe return of him who was to go to a still Farther North, the very top of the world, the Pole itself.

While waiting for Bartlett to return from his forced march, the main party had been at work, assorting dogs (by this time without much trouble, as only one was found utterly unfit to make progress), and rearranging loads, for the Captain had almost three hundred miles of sea-ice to negotiate before he would reach *terra firma*, and he had to have his food-supply arranged so that it would carry him to the land and back to the ship, and dogs in good enough condition to pull the loads, as well as enough sledges to bear his equipment. When he did come back to our camp, before the parting, he was perfectly satisfied, and with the same old confidence he swept his little party together and at three P. M., with a cheery "Good-by! Good Luck!" he was off. His Esquimo boys, attempting in English, too, gave us their "Good-bys." The least emotional of all of our partings; and this brave man, who had borne the brunt of all of the hardships, like the true-blue, dead-game, unconquerable hero that he was, set out to do the work that was left for him to do; to knit the broken strands of our upward trail together, so that we who were at his rear could follow in safety.

I have never heard the story of the return of Captain Bartlett in detail; his Esquimo boys were incapable of telling it, and Captain Bartlett is altogether too modest.

CHAPTER 15

THE POLE!

Captain Bartlett and his two boys had commenced their return journey, and the main column, depleted to its final strength, started northward. We were six: Peary, the commander, the Esquimos, Ootah, Egingwah, Seegloo and Ooqueah, and myself.

Day and night were the same. My thoughts were on the going and getting forward, and on nothing else. The wind was from the southeast, and seemed to push us on, and the sun was at our backs, a ball of livid fire, rolling his way above the horizon in never-ending day.

The Captain had gone, Commander Peary and I were alone (save for the four Esquimos), the same as we had been so often in the past years, and as we looked at each other we realized our position and we knew without speaking that the time had come for us to demonstrate that we were the men who, it had been ordained, should unlock the door which held the mystery of the Arctic. Without an instant's hesitation, the order to push on was given, and we started off in the trail made by the Captain to cover the Farthest North he had made and to push on over one hundred and thirty miles to our final destination.

The Captain had had rough going, but, owing to the fact that his trail was our track for a short time, and that we came to good going shortly after leaving his turning point, we made excellent distance without any trouble, and only stopped when we came to a lead barely frozen over, a full twenty-five miles beyond. We camped and waited for the strong southeast wind to force the sides of the lead together. The Esquimos had eaten a meal of stewed dog, cooked over a fire of wood from a discarded sledge, and, owing to their wonderful powers of recuperation, were in good condition; Commander Peary and myself, rested and invigorated by our thirty hours in the last camp, waiting for the return and departure of Captain Bartlett, were also in fine fettle, and accordingly the accomplishment of twenty-five miles of northward progress was not exceptional. With my proven ability in gauging distances, Commander Peary was ready to take the reckoning as I made it and he did not resort to solar observations until we were within a hand's grasp of the Pole.

The memory of those last five marches, from the Farthest North of Captain Bartlett to the arrival of our party at the Pole, is a memory of toil, fatigue, and exhaustion, but we were urged on and encouraged by our relentless commander, who was himself being scourged by the final lashings of the dominating influence that had controlled his life. From the land to 87° 48' north, Commander Peary had had the best of the going, for he had brought up the rear and had utilized the trail made by the preceding parties, and thus he had kept himself in the best of condition for the time when he made the spurt that brought him to the end of the race. From 87° 48' north, he kept in the lead and did his work in such a way as to convince me that he was still as good a man as he had ever been. We marched and marched, falling down in our tracks repeatedly, until it was impossible to go on. We were forced to camp, in spite of the impatience of the Commander, who found himself unable to rest, and who only waited long enough for us to relax into sound sleep, when he would wake us up and start us off again. I do not believe that he slept for one hour from April 2 until after he had loaded us up and ordered us to go back over our old trail, and I often think that from the instant when the order to return was given until the land was again sighted, he was in a continual daze.

Onward we forced our weary way. Commander Peary took his sights from the time our chronometer-watches gave, and I, knowing that we had kept on going in practically a straight line, was sure that we had more than covered the necessary distance to insure our arrival at the top of the earth.

It was during the march of the 3d of April that I endured an instant of hideous horror. We were crossing a lane of moving ice. Commander Peary was in the lead setting the pace, and a half hour later the four boys and myself followed in single file. They had all gone before, and I was standing and pushing at the upstanders of my sledge, when the block of ice I was using as a support slipped from underneath my feet, and before I knew it the sledge was out of my grasp, and I was floundering in the water of the lead. I did the best I could. I tore my hood from off my head and struggled frantically. My hands were gloved and I could not take hold of the ice, but before I could give the "Grand Hailing Sigh of Distress," faithful old Ootah had grabbed me by the nape of the neck, the same as he would have grabbed a dog, and with one hand he pulled me out of the water, and with the other hurried the team across.

He had saved my life, but I did not tell him so, for such occurrences are taken as part of the day's work, and the sledge he safeguarded was of much more importance, for it held, as part of its load, the Commander's sextant, the mercury, and the coils of piano-wire that were the essential portion of the scientific part of the expedition. My kamiks (boots of seal-skin) were stripped off, and the congealed water was beaten out of my bearskin trousers, and with a dry pair of kamiks, we hurried on to overtake the column. When we caught up we found the boys gathered around the Commander, doing their best to relieve him of his discomfort, for he had fallen into the water also, and while he was not complaining. I was sure that his bath had not been any more voluntary than mine had been.

When we halted on April 6, 1909, and started to build the igloos, the dogs and sledges having been secured, I noticed Commander Peary at work unloading his sledge and unpacking several bundles of equipment. He pulled out from under his *kooletah* (thick, fur outer-garment) a small folded package and unfolded it. I recognized his old silk flag, and realized that this was to be a camp of importance. Our different camps had been known as Camp Number One, Number Two, etc., but after the turning back of Captain Bartlett, the camps had been given names such as Camp Nansen, Camp Cagni, etc., and I asked what the name of this camp was to be—"Camp Peary"? "This, my boy, is to be Camp Morris K. Jesup, the last and most northerly camp on the earth." He fastened the flag to a staff and planted it firmly on the top of his igloo. For a few minutes it hung limp and lifeless in the dead calm of the haze, and then a slight breeze, increasing in strength, caused the folds to straighten out, and soon it was rippling out in sparkling color. The stars and stripes were "nailed to the Pole."

A thrill of patriotism ran through me and I raised my voice to cheer the starry emblem of my native land. The Esquimos gathered around and, taking the time from Commander Peary, three hearty cheers rang out on the still, frosty air, our dumb dogs looking on in puzzled surprise. As prospects for getting a sight of the sun were not good, we turned in and slept, leaving the flag proudly floating above us.

This was a thin silk flag that Commander Peary had carried on all of his Arctic journeys, and he had always flown it at his last camps. It was as glorious and as inspiring a banner as any battle-scarred, blood-stained standard of the world—and this badge of honor and courage was also blood-stained and battle-scarred, for at several places there were blank squares marking the spots where pieces had been cut out at each of the "Farthests" of its brave bearer, and left with the records in the cairns, as mute but eloquent witnesses of his achievements. At the North Pole a diagonal strip running from the upper left to the lower right corner was cut and this precious strip, together with a brief record, was placed in an empty tin, sealed up and buried in the ice, as a record for all time.

Commander Peary also had another American flag, sewn on a white ground, and it was the emblem of the "Daughters of the Revolution Peace Society"; he also had and flew the emblem of the Navy League, and the emblems of a couple of college fraternities of which he was a member.

It was about ten or ten-thirty A. M., on the 7th of April 1909, that the Commander gave the order to build a snow-shield to protect him from flying drift of the surface-snow. I knew that he was about to take an observation, and while we worked I was nervously apprehensive, for I felt that the end of our journey had come. When we handed him the pan of mercury the hour was within a very few minutes of noon. Laying flat on his stomach, he took the elevation and made the notes on a piece of tissue-paper at his head. With sun-blinded eyes, he snapped shut the *vernier* (a graduated scale that subdivides the smallest divisions on the sector of the circular scale of the sextant) and with the resolute squaring of his jaws, I was sure that he was satisfied, and I was confident that the journey had ended. Feeling that the time had come, I ungloved my right hand and went forward to congratulate him on the success of our eighteen years of effort, but a gust of wind blew something into his eye, or else the burning pain caused by his prolonged look at the reflection of the limb of the sun forced him to turn aside; and with both hands covering his eyes, he gave us orders to not let him sleep for more than four hours, for six hours later he purposed to take another sight about four miles beyond, and that he wanted at least two hours to make the trip and get everything in readiness.

I unloaded a sledge, and reloaded it with a couple of skins, the instruments, and a cooker with enough alcohol and food for one meal for three, and then I turned in to the igloo where my boys were already sound asleep. The thermometer registered 29° below zero. I fell into a dreamless sleep and slept for about a minute, so I thought, when I was awakened by the clatter and noise made by the return of Peary and his boys.

The Commander gave the word, "We will plant the stars and stripes—*at the North Pole!*" and it was done; on the peak of a huge paleocrystic floeberg the glorious banner was unfurled to the breeze, and as it snapped and crackled with the wind, I felt a savage joy and exultation. Another world's accomplishment was done and finished, and as in the past, from the beginning of history, wherever the world's work was done by a white man, he had been accompanied by a colored man. From the building of the pyramids and the journey to the Cross, to the discovery of the new world and the discovery of the North Pole, the Negro had been the faithful and constant companion of the Caucasian, and I felt all that it was possible for me to feel, that it was I, a lowly member of my race, who had been chosen by fate to represent it, at this, almost the last of the world's great *work*.

The four Esquimos who stood with Commander Peary at the North Pole, were the brothers, Ootah and Egingwah, the old campaigner, Seegloo, and the sturdy, boyish Ooqueah. Four devoted companions, blindly confident in the leader, they worked only that he might succeed and for the promise of reward that had been made before they had left the ship, which promise they were sure would be kept. Together with the faithful dogs, these men had insured the success of the master. They had all of the characteristics of the dogs, including the dogs' fidelity. Within their breasts lingered the same infatuations that Commander Peary seemed to inspire in all who were with him, and though frequently complaining and constantly requiring to be urged to do their utmost, they worked faithfully and willingly. Ootah, of my party, was the oldest, a married man, of about thirty-four years, and regarded as the best all around member of the tribe, a great hunter, a kind father, and a good provider. Owing to his strong character and the fact that he was more easily managed by me than by any of the others, he had been a member of my party from the time we left the ship. Without exaggeration, I can say that we had both saved each other's lives more than once, but it had all gone in as part of the day's work, and neither of us dwelt on our obligations to the other.

My other boy, Ooqueah, was a young man of about nineteen or twenty, very sturdy and stocky of build, and with an open, honest countenance, a smile that was "child-like and bland," and a character that *was* child-like and bland. It was alleged that the efforts of young Ooqueah were spurred on by the shafts of love, and that it was in the hopes of winning the hand of the demure Miss Anadore, the charming daughter of Ikwah, the first Esquimo of Commander Peary's acquaintance, that he worked so valiantly. His efforts were of an ardent character, but it was not due to the ardor of love as far as I could see, but to his desire to please and his anxiety to win the promised rewards that would raise him to the grade of a millionaire, according to Esquimo standards.

Commander Peary's boy, Egingwah, was the brother of my boy Ootah, also married and of good report in his community, and it was he who drove the Morris K. Jesup sledge.

If there was any sentiment among the Esquimos in regard to the success of the venture, Ootah and Seegloo by their unswerving loyalty and fidelity expressed it. They had been members of the "Farthest North party" in 1906, the party that was almost lost beyond and in the "Big Lead," and only reached the land again in a state of almost complete collapse. They were the ones who, on bidding Commander Peary farewell in 1906, when he was returning, a saddened and discouraged man, told him to be of good cheer and that when he came back again Ootah and Seegloo would go along, and stay until Commander Peary had succeeded, and they did. The cowardice of their fellow Esquimos at the "Big Lead" on this journey did not in the least demoralize them, and when they were absolutely alone on the trail, with every chance to turn back and return to the comfort, wife, and family, they remained steadfast and true, and ever northward guided their sledges.

CHAPTER 16

THE FAST TREK BACK TO LAND

*T*he long trail was finished, the work was done, and there was only left for us to return and tell the tale of the doing. Reaction had set in, and it was with quavering voice that Commander Peary gave the order to break camp. Already the strain of the hard upward-journey was beginning to tell, and after the first two marches back, he was practically a dead weight, but do not think that we could have gotten back without him, for it was due to the fact that he was with us, and that we could depend upon him to direct and order us, that we were able to keep up the break-neck pace that enabled us to cover three of our upward marches on one of our return marches, and we never forgot that he was still the heart and head of the party.

It was broad daylight and getting brighter, and accordingly I knew little fear, though I did think of the ghosts of other parties, flitting in spectral form over the ice-clad wastes, especially of that small detachment of the Italian expedition of the Duke D'Abruzzi, of which to this day neither track, trace, nor remembrance has ever been found. We crossed lead after lead, sometimes like a bareback rider in the circus, balancing on cake after cake of ice, but good fortune was with us all the way, and it was not until the land of recognizable character had been lifted that we lost the trail, and with the land in sight as an incentive, it was no trouble for us to gain the talus of the shore ice and find the trail again.

When we "hit the beach for fair" it was early in the morning of April 23, 1909, nearly seventeen days since we had left the Pole, but such a seventeen days of haste, toil, and misery as cannot be comprehended by the mind. We who experienced it, Commander Peary, the Esquimos, and myself, look back to it as to a horrid nightmare, and to describe it is impossible for me.

Commander Peary had taken the North Pole by conquest, in the face of almost insuperable natural difficulties, by the tremendous fighting-power of himself. The winning of the North Pole was a fight with nature; the way to the pole that had been covered and retraced by Commander Peary lay across the ever moving and drifting ice of the Arctic Ocean. For more than a hundred miles from Cape Columbia it was piled in heavy pressure ridges, ridge after ridge, some more than a hundred feet in height. In addition, open lanes of water held the parties back until the leads froze up again, and continually the steady drift of the ice carried us back on the course we had come, but due to his deathless ambition to know and to do, he had conquered. He had added to the sum of Earth's knowledge, and proven that the mind of man is boundless in its desire.

The long quest for the North Pole is over and the awful space that separated man from the *Ultima Thule* has been bridged. There is no more beyond; from Cape Columbia to

Cape Chelyuskin, the route northward to the Pole, and southward again to the plains of Asia, is an open book and the geographical mind is at rest.

We found the abandoned igloos of Crane City and realized that Captain Bartlett had reached the land safely. The damage due to the action of the storms was not material. We made the necessary repairs, and in a few minutes tea was boiled and rations eaten, and we turned in for sleep. For practically all of the two days following, that was what we did: sleep and eat; men and dogs thoroughly exhausted; and we slept the sleep of the just, without apprehensions or misgivings. Our toboggan from the Pole was ended.

Different from all other trips, we had not on this one been maddened by the pangs of hunger, but instead we felt the effects of lack of sleep, and brain- and body-fatigue. After reaching the land again, I gave a keen searching look at each member of the party, and I realized the strain they had been under. Instead of the plump, round countenances I knew so well, I saw lean, gaunt faces, seamed and wrinkled, the faces of old men, not those of boys, but in their eyes still shone the spark of resolute determination.

Commander Peary's face was lined and seamed, his beard was fully an inch in length, and his mustaches, which had been closely cropped before he left the ship, had again attained their full flowing length. His features expressed fatigue, but the heart-breaking look of sadness, that had clung to him since the failure of the 1906 expedition, had vanished. From his steel-gray eyes flashed forth the light of glorious victory, and though he always carried himself proudly, there had come about him an air of erect assurance that was exhilarating.

When I reached the ship again and gazed into my little mirror, it was the pinched and wrinkled visage of an old man that peered out at me, but the eyes still twinkled and life was still entrancing. This wizening of our features was due to the strain of travel and lack of sleep; we had enough to eat, and I have only mentioned it to help impress the fact that the journey to the Pole and back is not to be regarded as a pleasure outing, and our so-called jaunt was by no means a cake-walk.

Matthew Henson at ease, in work clothes, on deck, ca. 1908-09.
Courtesy of The Arctic Museum, Bowdoin College.

Matthew Henson on deck in furs at the front of a sledge, with companions Donald MacMillan, George Borup, and Tom Gushue, 1909. Courtesy of The Arctic Museum, Bowdoin College.

Four Eskimos at Cape Sheridan, 1909. This photograph, taken by Henson, appeared in the first edition of the autobiography of 1912. Courtesy of The Arctic Museum, Bowdoin College.

Matthew Henson in furs, on the deck of the SS Roosevelt, 1908-09.
Courtesy of The Arctic Museum, Bowdoin College.

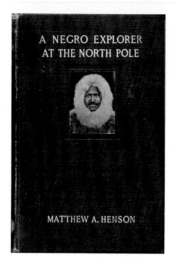

Henson's leather mitten. One of the pair of sealskin leather mittens is inscribed "Matthew A. Henson May 5-1934 To—Explorers Club… Worn by me from Cape Sheridan to it–North Pole April 8, 1909." The Explorers Club. Photograph by Judy Beisler, Mystic Seaport, Mystic CT, with the permission of The Explorers Club.

First edition of the autobiography. Matthew Alexander Henson, A Negro Explorer at the North Pole. With a Foreword by Robert E. Peary and an Introduction by Booker T. Washington. New York: Frederick A. Stokes Co., 1912. Photograph by Judy Beisler, Mystic Seaport, Mystic CT, with the permission of The Explorers Club.

Collage of printed ephemera. At the center is a "trade card" labeled "Matthew Henson: The World's Greatest Explorer," ca. 1909, from a painting by Albert Operti. From the 1980's and later: a "trade card," an envelope bearing the U.S. postage stamp with images of Peary and Henson from 1986, and a decorative magnet, in plastic, from Bowdoin College. **Courtesy of David H. and Deirdre C. Stam.**

Array of illustrated books for children on Matthew Henson. **Courtesy of David H. and Deirdre C. Stam.**

Henson with other members of The Explorers Club. To Henson's right is Vilhjalmur Stefansson and to his left, Peter Freuchen. **Photograph by Judy Beisler, Mystic Seaport, Mystic CT, with the permission of The Explorers Club.**

Bust of Henson by John LaFarge, created ca. 1953. **Photograph by Judy Beisler, Mystic Seaport, Mystic CT, with the permission of The Explorers Club.**

K119CC 3M NL PD

NEWYORK NY JAN 23 1953

EXPLORERS CLUB

10 WEST 72 ST NYK

AN ADMIRER OF MATTHEW HENSON WISHES PRESENTED TO THE EXPLORERS CLUB
A BUST OF MR.HENSON BY A DISTINGUISHED SCULPTOR, MR JOHN LA FARGE.
MR AVERELL HARRIMAN HAS CONSENTED TO MAKE PRESENTATION ON BEHALF OF
THE DONOR AND THE NATIONAL ASSOCIATION FOR THE ADVANCEMENT OF COLORED
PEOPLE. MR. HARRIMAN HAS INFORMED US THAT HE CAN DO SO ON MONDAY
FEBRUARY 9 AT 6 PM. WILL YOU TELEGRAPH US COLLECT IF EXPLORERS CLUB
WILL ACCEPT BUST AND IF THAT DATE IS AGREEABLE. WE WOULD ALSO
APPRECIATE YOUR INFORMING US OF SIZE OF AUDITORIUM SO WE MAY LIMIT
INVITATIONS TO CONFORM TO SEATING CAPACITY.

WALTER WHITE, SECY, NAACP 20 W. 40 ST NYC

848P

Telegram from the secretary of the NAACP requesting the opportunity to present LaFarge's bust of Henson to The Explorers Club.
Photograph by Judy Beisler, Mystic Seaport, Mystic CT, with the permission of The Explorers Club.

Matthew Henson statuette with U.S. flag and dog. Painted plaster, 5.25" tall, c. 2003. **Courtesy of David H. and Deirdre C. Stam.**

CHAPTER 17

SAFE ON THE *ROOSEVELT*—POOR MARVIN

*I*f you will remember, the journey from Cape Sheridan to Cape Columbia was with overloaded sledges in the darkness preceding the dawn of the Arctic day, mostly over rough going and up-hill, and now the tables were turned. It was broad day and down-hill with lightened sledges, so that we practically coasted the last miles from the twin peaks of Columbia to the low, slanting fore-shore of Sheridan and the *Roosevelt.* After the forty hours' rest at Cape Columbia, Commander Peary had his sledges loaded up, and with Egingwah and the best of the remaining dogs, he got away.

I was told I could remain at the camp for another twelve hours. A large and substantial cache of supplies had been dropped at Cape Columbia by various members of the expedition and when the Commander was gone, I gave the boys full permission to turn in and eat all they wanted, and I also gave the dogs all they could stuff, and it was not until all of us had gorged ourselves to repletion that I gave the order to *vamoose.* We were loaded to capacity, outward and inward, and we saw a bountiful supply still lying there, but we could not pack another ounce. It was early in the morning of April 25 when Peary started for the ship; it was about four or five hours later, about noon, when I gave the word, and Ootah,

Seegloo, Ooqueah, and myself left Crane City, Cape Columbia, Grant Land, for the last time.

We overtook the Commander at Point Moss, and we traveled with him to Cape Colan, where we camped. Peary continued on to Sail Harbor, and we stayed in our comfortable camp and rested. We again caught up with the Commander at Porter Bay, where we camped for a few hours. The following morning I rearranged the sledges and left two of them at Porter Bay. It was my intention to reach the ship on this evening. We made a short stop at Black Cliff Bay and had lunch, and without further interruption we traveled on and at about eight-forty-five P. M. we sighted the *Roosevelt*.

The sighting of the ship was our first view of home, and far away as she was, our acutely developed senses of smell were regaled with the appetizing odor of hot coffee, and the pungent aroma of tobacco-smoke, wafted to us through the clear, germ-free air. The Esquimo boys, usually excited on the slightest provocation, were surprisingly stolid and merely remarked, *"Oomiaksoah"* ("The ship") in quiet voices, until I, unable to control myself, burst forth with a loud "hip! hip! hurrah!" and with all that was left of my energy hurried my sledge in to the ship. We had been sighted almost as quickly as we had sighted the ship, and a party of the ship's crew came running out to meet us, and as we rushed on we were told about the safe arrival of Commander Peary, Bartlett, Borup, MacMillan, and Dr. Goodsell. Transported with elation and overjoyed to find myself once more safe among friends, I had rushed onward and as I recognized the different faces of the ship's company, I did not realize that some were missing.

Chief Wardwell was the first man to greet me, he photographed me as I was closing in on the ship, and with his strong right arm pulled me up over the side and hugged me to his bosom. "Good boy, Matt," he said; "too bad about Marvin," and then I knew that all was wrong and that it was not the time for rejoicing. I asked for Peary and I was told that he was all right. I saw Captain Bartlett and I knew that he was there; but where was Borup, where were MacMillan, Marvin, and where was Dr. Goodsell? Dr. Goodsell was right by my side, holding me up, and I realized that it was of him I was demanding to know of the others.

Reason had not left me, the bonds of sanity had not snapped, but for the time I was hysterical, and I only knew that all were well and safe excepting Marvin, who was drowned. A big mug of coffee was given to me, I drank a spoonful; a glass of spirits was handed me, I drank it all, and I was guided to my cabin, my fur clothes were taken off, and for the first time in sixty-eight days, I allowed myself to relax and I fell into a sleep.

When I awoke, I had the grandest feast imaginable set before me, and after eating, I had the most luxurious bath possible, and then some more to eat, and afterwards, some more sleep; then I shaved myself, combed my hair, and came out of the cabin and crossed over to the galley, and sat on a box and watched Charley at work. Then I thought of the dogs and went outside and found that they had been cared for. I wondered when the Commander would want to see me. All of the time the sailors and Charley and the Esquimo folks were keeping up a running fire of conversation, and I was able to gather from what they said that my dear, good friend, Professor Marvin, was indeed lost; that Peary had reached the *Roosevelt* about seven hours ahead of me; that Captain Bartlett was suffering with swollen legs and feet; that MacMillan and Borup with their own and Marvin's boys had gone to Cape Jesup; and that Pooadloonah and Panikpah had taken their families and returned to Esquimo land.

For days after I reached the *Roosevelt*, I did nothing but rest and eat. The strain was over and I had all but collapsed, but with constant eating and sleeping, I was quickly myself again. The pains and swellings of my limbs did not come as they had on all of the other returnings, and neither was Peary troubled. Captain Bartlett was the only one of the expedition that had been out on the sea-ice who felt any after effects. Every day, a few minutes after rising, he would notice that his ankle- knee- and hip-joints were swollen; and while the pain was not excessive, he was incapacitated for more than ten days, and he spent the most of his time in his cabin. When he came out of his cabin and did talk to me, it was only to compare notes and agree that our experiences proved that there was absolutely no question about our having discovered the Pole.

Captain Bartlett, Dr. Goodsell, Chief Wardwell, Percy—they could talk as they would; but the one ever-present thought in my mind was of Marvin, and of his death. I thought of him, and of his kindness to me; and the picture of his widowed mother, patiently waiting the return of her son, was before me all of the time. I thought of my own mother, whom I scarcely remembered, and I sincerely wished that it had been me who had been taken. When MacMillan and Borup returned, I learned all about the sad affair, from Kudlooktoo and Harrigan, and I felt had he been with civilized companions the sad story of Marvin's death would not have to be told.

On breaking camp he had gone on, leaving the boys to load up and follow him. They were going south to the land and the ship, and there was no need for him to stay with them, and when they came up to where he had disappeared, they saw the ice newly formed about him, his head and feet beneath, and nothing showing but the fur clothing of his back and shoulders. They made no effort to rescue him, and had they succeeded in getting his body out, there is little chance that they could have kept him alive, for the temperature was far below zero, and they knew nothing about restoring life to the drowned. No blame can be laid to his childish companions.

He died alone, and he passed into the great unknown alone, bravely and honorably. He is the last of earth's great martyrs; he is home; his work is done; he is where he longed to be; the Sailor is Home in the Sea. It is poor satisfaction to those that he left behind that his grave is the northern-most grave on the earth; but they realize that the sacrifice was not made in vain, for it was due to him that those who followed were able to keep the trail and reach the land again. The foolish boys, in accordance with Esquimo tradition, had unloaded all of Prof. Marvin's personal effects on the ice, so that his spirit should not follow them, and they hurried on back to land and to the ship, where they told their sad story.

Chapter 18

After Musk-Oxen
—The Doctor's Scientific Expedition

From the time of my arrival at the *Roosevelt*, for nearly three weeks, my days were spent in complete idleness. I would catch a fleeting glimpse of Commander Peary, but not once in all of that time did he speak a word to me. Then he spoke to me in the most ordinary, matter-of-fact way, and ordered me to get to work. Not a word about the North Pole or anything connected with it; simply, "There is enough wood left, and I would like to have you make a couple of sledges and mend the broken ones. I hope you are feeling all right." There was enough wood left and I made three sledges, as well as repaired those that were broken.

The Commander was still running things and he remained the commander to the last minute; nothing escaped him, and when the time came to slow-down on provisions, he gave the orders, and we had but two spare meals a day to sustain us. The whole expedition lived on travel rations from before the time we left Cape Sheridan until we had reached Sidney, N. S., and like the keen-fanged hounds, we were always ready and fit.

It was late in May when Prof. MacMillan and Mr. Borup, with their Esquimo companions, returned from Cape Jesup, where they had been doing highly important scientific work, taking soundings our on the sea-ice north of the cape as high as 84° 15' north, and also at the cape. They had made a trip that was record-breaking; they had visited the different cairns made by Lockwood and Brainard and by Commander Peary, and they had also captured and brought into the ship a musk-oxen calf; and they had most satisfactorily demonstrated their fitness as Arctic explorers, having followed the Commander's orders implicitly, and secured more than the required number of tidal-readings and soundings.

Prof. MacMillan, with Jack Barnes, a sailor, and Kud-looktoo, left for Fort Conger early in June, and continued the work of tidal-observations. They rejoined the *Roosevelt* just before she left Cape Sheridan. A little later in the month, Borup went to Clements Markham Inlet to hunt musk-oxen, and from there he went to Cape Columbia, where he erected the cairn containing the record of the last and successful expe-dition of the "Peary Arctic Club." The cairn was a substan-tial pile of rocks, surmounted by a strong oaken guide-post, with arms pointing "North 413 miles to the Pole"; "East, to Cape Morris K. Jesup, 275 miles"; "West to Cape Thomas H. Hubbard, 225 miles"; while the southern arm pointed south, but to no particular geographical spot; it was labeled "Cape Columbia." Underneath the arms of the guide-post, which had been made by Mate Gushue, was a small, glass-covered, box-like arrangement, in which was encased the record of Peary's successful journey to the Pole, and the roster of the expedition, my name included. From the crossbars, guys of galvanized wire were stretched and secured to heavy rocks, to help sustain the monument from the fury of the storms. Borup did good work, photographed the result, and the picture of the cairn, when exhibited, proved very satisfactory to the Commander.

Dr. Goodsell with two teams, and the Esquimo men, Keshungwah and Tawchingwah, left the ship on May 27, to hunt in the Lake Hazen and Ruggles River regions. They were successful in securing thirteen musk-oxen in that neighborhood, and in Bellows Valley they shot a number of the "Peary" caribou, the species *"Rangifer Pearyi,"* a distinct class of reindeer inhabiting that region.

On the return of Dr. Goodsell, he told of his fascinating experiences in that wonderland. Leaving the *Roosevelt*, he had turned inland at Black Cliff Bay. Past the glaciers he went with his little party, down the Bellows Valley to the Ruggles River, an actual stream of clear-running water, alive with the finest of salmon trout. Adopting the Esquimo methods, he fished for these speckled beauties with joyful success. Here he rounded up and shot the herd of musk-oxen, and here he bagged his caribou. He was in a hunter's paradise and made no haste to return, but crossed overland to Discovery Harbor and the barn-like structure of Fort Conger, the headquarters of General Greely's "Lady Franklin Bay Expedition" of 1882–1883. Professor MacMillan was on his way to Fort Conger and it was with much surprise, on arriving there, that he found that

Dr. Goodsell had reached it an hour before him. It was an unexpected meeting and quite a pleasure to the Professor to find the Doctor there, ready to offer him the hospitality of the fort.

Dr. Goodsell returned to the *Roosevelt* on June 15, with a load of geological, zoological, and botanical specimens almost as heavy as the loads of meat and skins he brought in. He was an ardent scientist, and viewed nearly every situation and object from the view-point of the scientist. Nothing escaped him; a peculiar form of rock or plant, the different features of the animal life, all received his close and eager attention, and he had the faculty of imparting his knowledge to others, like the born teacher that he was. He evinced an eager interest in the Esquimos and got along famously with them.

His physical equipment was the finest; a giant in stature and strength, but withal the gentlest of men having an even, mellow disposition that never was ruffled. In the field the previous spring he had accompanied the expedition beyond the "Big Lead" to 84° 29', and with the strength of his broad shoulders he had pickaxed the way.

On account of his calm, quiet manner I had hesitated to form an opinion of him at first, but you can rest assured this was a "Tenderfoot" who made good.

During this time I left the ship on short hunting trips, but I was never away from the ship for more than ten or twelve hours.

On July 1 quite a lead was opened in the channel south from Cape Sheridan to Cape Rawson. The ice was slowly moving southward, and the prospects for freeing the *Roosevelt* and getting her started on her homeward way were commencing to brighten. The following day a new lead opened much nearer shore, and on July 3 the Esquimos, who had been out hunting, returned from Black Cliff Bay, without game, but with the good news that as far south as Dumb Bell Bay there stretched a lead of open water. July 4, a new lead opened very close to the *Roosevelt*. The spring tides, with a strong southerly wind, had set in so very much earlier, three years before, that on July 4, 1906, the *Roosevelt* had been entirely free of ice, with clear, open water for quite a distance to the south; but this year the ship was still completely packed in the ice, and furthermore she was listed at the same angle as during the winter.

On July 5, I was detailed to help Gushue repair the more or less damaged whale-boats. The heavy and solidly packed snow of the winter had stove them in. On July 6, the anniversary of our departure from New York a year before, the greater part of the day was spent in pumping water from the top of a heavy floeberg into the ship's boilers. This work was not completed until the morning of the 7th, when the fires were started. Due to the cold, the process of getting up steam was slow work. The ice had been breaking up daily, new leads were noticed, and on this day, July 7, a new lead opened at a distance of fifty yards from the ship, and open water stretched as far south as the eye could see. All hands were put to work reloading the supplies that had been placed on shore the fall previous, for it was easy to see that the time for departure was at hand.

With the boilers in order, an attempt was made to revolve the shaft, but the propeller was too severely frozen in the ice to move, and so Captain Bartlett got out the dynamite and succeeded in freeing the bronze blades.

From the 10th of July to the 13th, a fierce storm raged, clouds of freeing spray broke over the ship, incasing her in a coat of icy mail, and the tempest forced all of the ice out of the lower end of the channel and beyond as far as the eye could see, but the *Roosevelt* still remained surrounded by ice.

The morning of the 15th, a smart breeze from the north-east was blowing, and proved of valuable assistance to us, for it caused the huge block of ice that were surrounding the ship to loosed their hold, and for the first time since October, 1908, the *Roosevelt* righted herself to an even keel.

By this time all of our supplies had been loaded and stored, and from the crows-nest a stretch of open water could be seen as far as Cape Rawson. From there to Cape Union the ice was packed solid.

CHAPTER 19

THE *ROOSEVELT* STARTS FOR HOME
—ESQUIMO VILLAGES—NEW DOGS AND
NEW DOG FIGHTS

*I*t was two-thirty P. M., July 17, 1909, that the *Roosevelt* pointed her bow southward and we left our winter quarters and Cape Sheridan. We were on our journey home, all hands as happy as when, a year previous, we had started on our way north, with the added satisfaction of complete success. The ship had steamed but a short distance, when, owing to the rapidly drifting ice in the channel, she had to be made fast to a floeberg. At ten-thirty P. M., the lines were loosed and a new start made. Without further incident, we reached Black Cape.

In rounding the cape the ship encountered a terrific storm, and it was with the greatest difficulty that she made any headway. The storm increased and the *Roosevelt* had to remain in the channel, surrounded by the tightly wedged floes, at the mercy of the wind. The gale continued until the evening of the 20th. The constant surging back and forth of the channel-pack, with the spring tides and the several huge masses of ice, which repeatedly crashed against the ship's sides, caused a delay of twelve days in Robeson Channel opposite Lincoln Bay. Throughout the width of the entire channel nothing could be seen but small pools of open water; two seals were seen sporting in one of these pools, and one of the Esquimos attempted to kill them, but his aim proved false.

It was not until the 25th that the ship was able to move of her own free will, small leads having opened in close proximity to her. Ootah shot a seal in one of the leads, and also harpooned a narwhal, but he did not succeed in securing either. His brother Egingwah on the following day shot two seals and harpooned a narwhale, and he secured all three of his prizes. The Esquimos had a grand feast off the skin of the narwhal, which they esteem as a great delicacy.

By the 27th the *Roosevelt* had drifted as far south as Wrangell Bay, and it was here that Slocum (Inighito) shot and secured a hood-seal, which weighed over six hundred pounds, and seal-steaks were added to the bill-of-fare.

The snow storms of the two days ceased on the 28th, and when the weather cleared sufficiently for us to ascertain our whereabouts, we were much surprised to find that we had drifted back north, opposite Lincoln Bay. During the day the wind shifted to the north. Again we drifted southward, until, just off Cape Beechey, the narrowest part of Robeson Channel, a lead stretching southward for a distance of five miles was sighted, and into this open water the ship steamed until the lead terminated in Kennedy Channel, opposite Lady Franklin Bay, where the *Roosevelt* was ice-bound until August 4, drifting with the pack until we were in a direct line with Cape Tyson and Bellot Isle. Three seals were captured, one a hood-seal weighing 624 pounds, being eight feet eleven inches in length; the other two were small ring-seals.

By ten A. M. of the 4th, the ice had slackened so considerably that the *Roosevelt*, under full steam, set out and rapidly worked her way down Kennedy Channel. From Crozier Island to Cape D'Urville she steamed through practically open water, but a dense fog compelled us to make fast to a large floe when almost opposite Cape Albert. It was not until one A. M. of the 7th, despite several attempts, that the ship got clear and steamed south again. Several small leads were noticed and numerous narwhals were seen, but none were captured.

At three-thirty A. M., when nearing Cape Sabine, we observed that the barometer had dropped to 29.73. A storm was coming, and every effort was made to reach Payer Harbor, but before half of the distance had been covered, the storm broke with terrific violence. The force of the gale was such that, while swinging the boats inboard, we were drenched and thoroughly chilled by the sheets of icy spray, which saturated us and instantly froze. The *Roosevelt* was blown over to starboard until the rails were submerged. To save her, she was steered into Buchanan Bay, under the lee of the cliffs, where she remained until the morning of August 8.

At an early hour, we steamed down Buchanan Bay, passed Cocked Hat Island, and a little later, Cape Sabine. At Cape Sabine was located Camp Clay, the starvation camp of the Lady Franklin Bay expedition of 1881–1883, where the five survivors of the twenty-three members of the expedition were rescued.

We entered Smith Sound. Instead of sailing on to Etah, Peary ordered the ship into Whale Sound, in order that walrus-hunting could be done, so that the Esquimos should have a plentiful supply of meat for the following winter. Three walrus were captured, when a storm sprang up with all of the suddenness of storms in this neighborhood, and the ship crossed over from Cape Alexander to Cape Chalon. Cape Chalon is a favorite resort of the Esquimos, and is known as Peter-ar-wick, on account of the walrus that are to be found here during the months of February and March.

At Nerke, just below Cape Chalon, we found the three Esquimo families of Ahsayoo, Tungwingwah, and Ted-dylingwah, and it was from these people that we learned of Dr. Cook's safe return from Ellesmere Land. In spite of the fact that the *Roosevelt* was overloaded with dogs, paraphernalia, and Esquimos, these three families were taken aboard.

With them were several teams of dogs. The dogs aboard ship were the survivors of the pack that had been with us all throughout the campaign, and a number of litters of puppies that had been whelped since the spring season. Our dogs were well acquainted with each other and dog fights were infrequent and of little interest, but the arrival of the first dog of the new party was the signal for the grandest dog fight I have ever witnessed. I feel justified in using the language of the fairy Ariel, in Shakespeare's "Tempest": "Now is Hell empty, and all the devils are here."

Backward and forward, the foredeck of the ship was a howling, snarling, biting, yelping, moving mass of fury, and it was a long round of fully ten or fifteen minutes before the two king dogs of the packs got together, and then began the battle for supremacy of the pack. It lasted for some time. It would have been useless to separate them. They would decide sooner or later, and it was better to have it over, even if one or both contestants were killed. At length the fight was ended; our old king dog, Nalegaksoah, the champion of the pack, and the laziest dog in it, was still the king. After vanquishing his opponent and receiving humble acknowledgments, King Nalegaksoah went stamping up and down before the pack and received the homage due him; the new dogs, whining and fawning and cringingly submissive, bowed down before him.

The chief pleasure of the Esquimo dogs is fighting; two dogs, the best of friends, will hair-pull and bite each other for no cause whatever, and strange dogs fight at sight; teammates fight each other on the slightest of provocations; and it seems as though sometimes the fights are held for the purpose of educating the young. When a fight is in progress, it is the usual sight to see several mother dogs, with their litters, occupying ring-side seats. I have often wondered what chance a cat would stand against an Esquimo dog.

The ship kept on, and I had turned in and slept, and on arising had found that we had reached a place called

Igluduhomidy, where a single family was located. Living with this family was a very old Esquimo, Merktoshah, the oldest man in the whole tribe, and not a blood-relation to any member of it. He had crossed over from the west coast of Smith Sound the same year that Hall's expedition had wintered there, and has lived there ever since. He had been a champion polar bear and big game hunter, and though now a very old man, was still vigorous and valiant, in spite of the loss of one eye.

We stopped at Kookan, the most prosperous of the Esquimo settlements, a village of five tupiks (skin tents), housing twenty-four people, and from there we sailed to the ideal community of Karnah. Karnah is the most delightful spot on the Greenland coast. Situated on a greatly southward sloping knoll are the igloos and tupiks, where I have spent many pleasant days with my Esquimo friends and learned much of the folk-lore and history. Lofty mountains, sublime in their grandeur, overtower and surround this place, and its only exposure is southward toward the sun. In winter its climate is not severe, as compared with other portions of this country, and in the perpetual daylight of summer, life here is ideal. Rivulets of clear, cold water, the beds of which are grass- and flower-covered, run down the sides of the mountains and, but for the lack of trees, the landscape is as delightful as anywhere on earth.

CHAPTER 20

Two Narrow Escapes
—Arrival at Etah—Harry Whitney
—Dr. Cook's Claims

*F*rom Karnah the *Roosevelt* sailed to Itiblu, where hunting-parties secured thirty-one walrus and one seal. By the 11th of August we had reached the northern shore of Northumberland Island, where we were delayed by storm. It was shortly before noon of this day that we barely escaped another fatal calamity.

Chief Wardwell, while cleaning the rifle of Commander Peary, had the misfortune to have the piece explode while in his hands. From some unknown cause a cartridge was discharged, the projectile pierced two thick partitions of inch-and-a-half pine, and penetrated the cabin occupied by Professor MacMillan, and Mr. Borup. The billet of that bullet was the shoulder and forearm of Professor MacMillan, who at the time was sound asleep in his berth. He had been lying with his arm doubled and his head resting on his hand. A half inch nearer and the bullet would have entered his brain.

As is always the case with narrow escapes, I, too, had a narrow escape, for that same bullet entered the partition on its death-dealing mission at identically the same spot where a few minutes previously *my* head had rested. Dr. Goodsell was quickly aroused, he attended Professor MacMillan, and in a short time he diagnosed the case as a "gun-shot wound." Finding no bones broken, or veins or arteries open, he soon had the Professor bandaged and comfortable.

At the time of the accident to Professor MacMillan the ship was riding at anchor, but with insufficient slack-way, so in the afternoon, when the excitement had abated, Captain Bob decided to give the ship more chain, for a storm was imminent, and he gave the order accordingly. The boatswain, in his haste to execute the order, and overestimating the amount of chain in the locker, permitted all of it to run overboard. We were in a predicament, with the storm upon us, no anchor to hold the boat, and a savage, rocky shore on which we were in danger of being wrecked. There was a small five-hundred-pound anchor with a nine-inch cable of about one hundred and fifty fathoms remaining, which was repeatedly tried, but the ship was too much for this feather-weight anchor, and dragged it at will. Commander Peary, with his usual foresight, had ordered steam as soon as the approach of the storm was noticed, and now that the steam was up, he ordered that the ship be kept head-on, and steam up and down the coast until the storm abated. The storm lasted until the night of August 13, and the best part of the following day was spent by two boat-crews of twelve men, in grappling for the lost anchor and chain, and not until they had secured it and restored it once more to its locker were they permitted to rest. With the anchor secure, walrus-hunting commenced afresh, and on the ice-floes between Hakluyt and Northumberland Islands thirty more walrus were secured.

On August 16, the *Roosevelt* steamed back to Karnah, and the Esquimo people who intended living there for the following winter were landed. A very large supply of meat was landed also; in addition to the meat quite a number of useful presents, hatchets, knives, needles, some boards for the making and repairing of sledges, and some wood for lance- and harpoon-staves, and a box full of soap were landed. This inventory of presents may seem cheap and paltry to you, but to these natives such presents as we made were more appreciated than the gift of many dollars would be by a poverty-stricken family in this country. With the materials that Commander Peary furnished would be made the weapons of the chase, the tools of the seamstress, and the implements of the home-maker. The Esquimos have always known how to utilize every factor furnished by nature, and what has been given by the Commander has been given with the simple idea of helping them to make their life easier, and proves again the axiom, "The Lord helps those who help themselves."

After disembarking the Karnah contingent, the ship steamed to Etah, arriving there on the afternoon of August 17. As the *Roosevelt* was entering the harbor of Etah, all hands were on deck and on the lookout, for it was here that we were again to come in touch with the world we had left behind a year before. A large number of Esquimos were running up and down the shore, but there was no sign of the expected ship. Quickly a boat was lowered, and I saw to it that I was a member of the crew of that boat, and when we reached the beach the first person to greet me was old Panikpah, greasy, smiling, and happy as if I were his own son. I quickly recognized my old friend Pooadloonah, who greeted me with a merry laugh, and my misgivings as to the fate of this precious pair were dispelled. If you will remember, Panikpah and Pooadloonah were the two Esquimos who found, when on our Poleward journey, just about the time we had struck the "Big Lead," that there were a couple of fox-traps, or something like that, that they had forgotten to attend to, and that it was extremely necessary for them to go back and square up their accounts. Here they were, fat, smiling, and healthy; and I apprehend somewhat surprised to see us, but they bluffed it out well.

Murphy and the young man Pritchard were also here. Murphy and Pritchard were the members of the crew who had been left here to guard the provisions of the expedition, and to trade with the Esquimos. Another person also was there to greet us; but who had kept himself alive and well by his own pluck an clear grit, and who reported on meeting the Commander of having had a most satisfactory and enjoyable experience. I refer to Mr. Harry Whitney, the young man from New Haven, Conn., who had elected at the last hour, the previous autumn, to remain at Etah, to hunt the big game of the region. When the *Roosevelt* had sailed north from Etah, the previous August, he had been left absolutely alone; the *Erik* had sailed for home, and there was no way out of this desolute land for him until the relief ship came north the following year, or the *Roosevelt* came south to take him aboard. His outfit and equipment were sufficient for him and complete, but he had shared it with the natives until it was exhausted, and after that he had reverted to the life of the aborigines. When the *Roosevelt* reached Etah, Mr. Whitney was an Esquimo; but within one hour, he had a bath, a shave, and a hair-cut, and was the same mild-mannered gentleman that we had left there in the fall. He had gratified his ambitions in shooting musk-oxen, but he had not killed a single polar bear.

At Etah there were two boys, Etookahshoo and Ahpellah, boys about sixteen or seventeen years old, who had been with Dr. Cook for a year, or ever since he had crossed the channel to Ellesmere Land and returned again. These boys are the two he claims accompanied him to the North Pole. To us, up there at Etah, such a story was so ridiculous and absurd that we simply laughed at it. We knew Dr. Cook and his abilities; he had been the surgeon on two of Peary's expeditions and, aside from his medical ability, we had no faith in him whatever. He was not even good for a day's work, and the idea of his making such an astounding claim as having reached the Pole was so ludicrous that, after our laugh, we dropped the matter altogether.

On account of the world-wide controversy his story has caused, I will quote from my diary the impressions noted in regard to him:

"August 17, 1909, Etah, North Greenland.

"Mr. Harry Whitney came aboard with the boatswain and the cabin-boy, who had been left here last fall on our way to Cape Sheridan. Murphy is the boatswain and Pritchard the boy, both from Newfoundland, and they look none the worse for wear, in spite of the long time they have spent here. Mr. Whitney is the gentleman who came up on the *Erik* last year, and at the last moment decided to spend the winter with the natives. He had a long talk with the Commander before we left for the north, and has had quite a lengthy session with him since. I learn that Dr. Cook came over from Ellesmere Land with his two boys, Etookahshoo and Ahpellah, and in a confidential conversation with Mr. Whitney made the statement that he had reached the North Pole. Professor Mac-Millan and I have talked to his two boys and have learned that there is no foundation in fact for such a statement, and the Captain and others of the expedition have questioned them, and if they were out on the ice of the Arctic Ocean it was only for a very short distance, not more than twenty or twenty-five miles. They boys are positive in this statement, and my own boys, Ootah and Ooqueah, have talked to them also, and get the same replies. It is a fact that they had a very hard time and were reduced to low limits, but they have not been any distance north, and the Commander and the rest of us are in the humor to regard Mr. Whitney as a person who has been hoodwinked. We know Dr. Cook very well and also his reputation, and we know that he was never good for a hard days work; in fact he was not up to the average, and he is no hand at all in making the most of his resources. He probably has spun this yarn to Mr. Whitney and the boatswain to make himself look big to them.

"The Commander will not permit Mr. Whitney to bring any of the Dr. Cook effects aboard the *Roosevelt* and they have been left in a cache on shore. Koolootingwah is here again, after his trip to North Star Bay with Dr. Cook, and tells an amusing story of his experience."

It is only from a sense of justice to Commander Peary and those who were with him that I have mentioned Dr. Cook. The outfitting of the hunting expedition of Mr. Bradley was well known to us. Captain Bartlett had directed it and had advised and arranged for the purchase of the Schooner *John R. Bradley* to carry the hunting party to the region where big game of the character Mr. Bradley wished to hunt could be found. We knew that Dr. Cook was accompanying Mr. Bradley, but we had no idea that the question of the discovery of the North Pole was to be involved.

I have reason to be grateful to Dr. Cook for favors received; I lived with his folks while I was suffering with my eyes, due to snow blindness, but I feel that all of the debts of gratitude have been liquidated by my silence in this controversy, and I will have nothing more to say in regard to him or to his claims.

CHAPTER 21

ETAH TO NEW YORK
—COMING OF MAIL AND REPORTERS
—HOME!

$\mathcal{A}$ t Etah we expected to meet the relief ship. Sixty tons of coal and a small quantity of provisions had been left there during the previous summer, to be used by us on our homeward voyage. This coal was loaded on board and the Esquimos who desired to remain at Etah were landed. Just at the time we were ready to sail a heavy storm of wind and snow blew up, and it was not until six P. M. on the 20th that we left the harbor. Farewells had been said to the Esquimos, all that had been promised them for faithful services had been given to them, and we commenced the final stage of our journey home.

From Etah, August 20, the ship sailed along the coast, landing Esquimos at the different settlements, and on the 23rd of August at two A. M., we met the Schooner *Jeanie*, of St. John, N. F., commanded by Samuel Bartlett. The schooner was supplied with provisions and coal for the relief of the *Roosevelt*, and was executing the plan of the Peary Arctic Club.

There was mail aboard her and we had our first tidings of home and friends in a twelve-month. From newspaper clippings I learned that the British Antarctic Expedition, commanded by Sir Ernest H. Shackleton, had reached within 111 miles of the South Pole.

The mail contained good news for all but one of us. Mr. Borup, in his bunk above the Professor's, read his letters, and in the course of his reading was heard to emit a deep sigh then to utter an agonizing groan. Prof. MacMillan, thinking that Borup had received bad news indeed, endeavored to console him, and at the same time asked what was the bad news, feeling sure it could be nothing less than the death of Colonial Borup or some other close relative of his.

"What is the matter, George? Tell me."

"HARVARD BEAT YALE!"

The *Roosevelt*, accompanied by her consort, sailed south to North Star Bay and while entering the harbor ran ashore. Late in the afternoon, however, the rising tide floated her. While waiting for the tide, a party of six, I among the number, went ashore and visited the Danish Missionary settlement established there, the Esquimos acting as our interpreters, we being unable to speak Danish and the missionaries being unable to speak English. It was in North Star Bay that the coal and provisions from the *Jeanie* were transferred to the *Roosevelt*.

Aboard the *Jeanie*, there was a young Esquimo man, Mene, who for the past twelve years had lived in New York City, but, overcome by a strong desire to live again in his own country, had been sent north by his friends in the States. He was almost destitute, having positively nothing in the way of an equipment to enable him to withstand the rigors of the country, and was no more fitted for the life he was to take up than any boy of eighteen or twenty would be, for he was but a little boy when he first left North Greenland. However, Commander Peary ordered that he be given a plentiful supply of furs to keep him warm, food, ammunition and loading outfit, traps and guns, but, I believe, he would have gladly returned with us, for it was a wistful farewell he made, and an Esquimo's farewell is usually very barren of pathos.

Mr. Whitney transferred his augmented equipment to the *Jeanie*, intending to remain with her down the Labrador, for her Captain had agreed to use every effort to help Mr. Whitney secure at least one polar bear.

Cape York was reached on the morning of August 25, and from the two Esquimo families, living at the extreme point of the Cape, we obtained the mail which had been left there by Captain Adams of the Dundee Whaling Fleet *Morning Star*. Our letters, although they bore no more recent a date than that of March 23, 1909, were eagerly read.

At Cape York we landed the last of the Esquimos. The decks were now cleared. The boats were securely lashed in their davits, and nine A. M., August 26, in a gale of wind, the *Roosevelt* put out to sea, homeward-bound, but not yet out of danger, for the gale increased so considerably that the *Roosevelt* was forced to lay to under reefed foresail, in the lee of the middle pack, until the 29th, when the storm subsided and the ship got under way again.

On September 4 the Labrador was sighted. Under full steam we passed the Farmyard, a group of small islands which lie off the coast.

We arrived at Turnavik at seven-thirty P. M. Once again we saw signs of civilization. The men and women appeared in costumes of the Twentieth Century instead of the fur garments of the Esquimos. Here we loaded nineteen tons of coal. Here we feasted on fresh codfish, fresh vegetables, and other appetizing foods to which our palates had long been strangers.

You know the rest, for from Turnavik to Indian Harbor was only a few hours' sailing.

At Indian Harbor was located the wireless telegraph station from where Commander Peary flashed to the civilized world his laconic message, "Stars and Stripes nailed to the North Pole."

Within half an hour of our arrival, the British cutter *Fiona* entered the harbor and the officers came aboard the *Roosevelt*. Thereafter for every hour there was continuous excitement and reception of visitors.

On September 13th the steamer *Douglas H. Thomas*, of Sydney, C.B., arrived, having on board two representatives of the Associated Press, accompanied by Mr. Rood, a representative of *Harper's Magazine*.

The next day the cable-boat *Tyrian* arrived, with seventeen newspaper reporters, five photographers, and one stenographer. The *Tyrian* anchored outside the harbor and in five life-boats the party was brought aboard the *Roosevelt.* As they rowed they cheered, and when they sighted Commander Peary three ringing cheers and a tiger were given. The newspaper men requested an interview with the Commander. He granted their request, at the same time suggesting that they accompany him ashore to a fish-loft at the end of the pier, where there would be more room than aboard the ship. Accompanied by the members of the expedition, the Commander and the reporters left the ship. Arriving at the loft Commander Peary sat on some fishnets at the rear end of the loft, some of the reporters sat on barrels and nets, others squatted on the floor. They formed a semi-circle around him and eagerly listened to the first telling of his stirring story.

Before leaving Battle Harbor, we received a visit from the great missionary, Dr. Grenfell, the effect of whose presence was almost like a benediction.

On the morning of the 18th we left Battle Harbor accompanied by the tug *Douglas H. Thomas,* amidst the salutes of the many vessels and boats in the harbor and the cannon on the hill.

Through the Straits of Belle Isle we steamed, with a fair wind and a choppy sea. In the meantime I was busily engaged in making a strip to sew upon a large American flag. This was a board white bar which was to extend from the upper right to the lower left corner of the flag, with the words "North Pole" sewed on it.

About six A. M. on the 21st, a large white, steam-yacht was seen approaching, flying an American flag from her fore-mast and the English flag from the mizzenmast. We were close enough to her to distinguish Mrs. Peary and the children on board. A boat was quickly lowered from the yacht and the Peary family soon united aboard the *Roosevelt*.

All kinds of sailing craft now met the *Roosevelt* and by them she was escorted into the harbor of Sydney, C. B. Whistles were blown, thousands of people lined the shores of the harbor, cheering enthusiastically and waving flags, and as the *Roosevelt* was moored alongside the pier, a delegation of schoolgirls met the Commander, made an address, and presented him with a magnificent bouquet. The streets were gorgeously decorated and a holiday had been declared. A ripe, royal welcome was accorded the *Roosevelt* and the members of the expedition. Visitors boarded the ship and looted suc-cessfully for souvenirs.

It was at Sydney that the expedition commenced to disband. Commander Peary and his family returned to the United States via railroad-train.

The *Roosevelt* left Sydney on September 22 for New York City. A stop was made at Eagle Island, in Casco Bay, off the coast of Maine, where is located the summer home of Com-mander Peary, and here we landed most of his paraphernalia, some sledges and dogs. From Eagle Island we steamed direct to Sandy Hook, reaching there at noon on October 2. The next day the *Roosevelt* took her place with the replica of those two historic ships, the *Half Moon* and the *Clermont*, in the lead of the great naval parade.

And now my story is ended; it is a tale that is told. "Now is Othello's occupation gone."

I long to see them all again! the brave, cheery companions of the trail of the North. I long to see again the lithe figure of my Commander! and to hear again his clear, ringing voice urging and encouraging me onward, with his "Well done, my boy." I want to be with the party when they reach the untrod shores of Crocker Land; I yearn to be with those who reach the South Pole, the lure of the Arctic is tugging at my heart, to me the trail is calling!

"The Old Trail!
The Trail that is always New!"

Appendix

NOTES ON THE ESQUIMOS

The origin of the Esquimos is not known to a certainty. In color they are brown, their hair is heavy, straight, coarse, and black. In appearance they are short, fat, and well-developed; and they bear a strong resemblance to the Mongolian race.

Among the men of this tribe, quarrels and fights very rarely occur; but it is a very noticeable fact that while the men of the tribe do not make war on each other, the man of the family will, at the least provocation on the part of his better-half, without hesitation apply brute force to show his authority.

The tribe of these, the North Greenland Esquimos, numbers two hundred and eighteen.

Great interest was shown by the men when working implements, such as we used on board ship, were shown them. Eagerly they listened while the uses of many of these tools were explained to them. The women also showed great interest in any article that was foreign to them. They have a special liking for fancy beads of the smaller variety.

The Esquimos show a great capacity for imitation. They have also a marked sense of humor.

An Esquimo's sense of imitation is so keen that it is only necessary for him to observe a sledge-maker at work but once, when the same type of sledge will be reproduced in a very short time. On my last trip north, I noticed that the shirts worn by the Esquimos were similar and cut to our own. In 1906, the style had been entirely different.

The Esquimos show no desire to acquire the English language. With the exception of Kudlooktoo and Inighito, none of the tribe could speak English intelligently. The Esquimos' vocabulary is a complication of prefixes and suffixes, and many words in his language are very hard to pronounce.

The *tupiks* (tents) are made of seal-skin, and are used in summer. The igloos are built of snow, and are used in winter. A few igloos built of bowlders can be seen. The workmanship of this latter type of igloos is necessarily crude, for the bowlders are used in the rough state. On entering the *tuscoonah* (entrance), a bed-platform of stones five feet long, and six feet wide, confronts one. On each side of this platform are seen smaller platforms, each holding a *koodlah* (fire-pot).

This *koodlah* is made of a stone so soft that before it comes in contact with fire it can easily be cut with a knife. The name given by the Esquimos to it is *okeyoah*. Cooking utensils are first formed in the desired shape, then heat is applied, as a result of which the stone quickly hardens. The method of cooking as employed by the Esquimos is to suspend the *kool-eesoo* (cooking-pot) over the *koodlah* (fire-pot). The *koodlah* is the only means by which light can be secured in an Esquimo igloo. As fuel, the blubber of the narwhal is used.

The clothing of the male Esquimo consists of a *kooletah* (deerskin coat with hood attached) *nanookes* (foxskin trousers) and *kamiks* (sealskin boots); that of the female Esquimo, a *kopetah* (foxskin coat with hood attached) *nanookes* (foxskin trousers) and hip length *kamiks* (sealskin boots). The shirts of the male and female Esquimo are made from the skin of the auks, and one hundred and fifty of these little birds are used in the manufacture of one shirt.

The largest Esquimo family known among the North Greenland tribe, numbers six; as a rule, an Esquimo family rarely outnumbers three. An Esquimo family is not stationary. Rarely does a family remain in one place longer than one season, which is nine months. The principal reason for this constant moving is the scarcity of game; for after a season of hunting in one place, game becomes very scarce; and there is no other alternative but for the family to move on. Transportation is by means of sledges drawn by a team of dogs. Alcoholic drinks are not known among this tribe; but, of late, tobacco is extensively used. Previous to 1902, before the arrival of the Danes, tobacco was an unknown quantity.

The cleanliness of the Esquimos leaves room for much improvement.

With reference to their morals, strictly speaking they are markedly lax. The wife of an Esquimo is held in no higher esteem than are the goods and chattels of the household. She may at any time be loaned, borrowed, sold, or exchanged. They have no marriage ceremony.

The amusements of the Esquimos are few. Tests of strength and endurance occur between the men of the tribe; and visits are paid to the various settlements, during the long winter nights; and songs and choruses are sung, accompanied by a kind of tambourine which is made from the bladder of a walrus or seal, and stretched across the antlers of a reindeer.

The Esquimos are a very superstitious people. In the event of a fatal illness, the victim, just before death, is removed to a place outside the igloo, for should death enter the igloo that dwelling would instantly be destroyed. If the deceased be a man, he is rolled up in a sealskin, and strips of rawhide are lashed around the body to keep the skin intact. He is then carried to his last resting place. A low stone structure is built around the body to protect it from the foxes. His sledge, containing all his belongings, is placed close beside this structure, and his dogs harnessed to his sledge are strangled, and stretched their full length, with their forepaws extended. In the event of the deceased being a woman, her cooking utensils are placed beside her, and should she be the mother of a very young infant, its life is taken. In the case of a widower, the bereaved Esquimo remains in the igloo for three days, during which time a new suit of wearing apparel is made, and worn by him, and all clothing made by the deceased, is, by him, destroyed. His term of mourning now being ended, the

Esquimo, without more ado, takes unto himself a new wife. Members of the tribe who have the same name as the deceased have to change that name until the arrival of a new-born babe, to whom the name is given, whereby the ban is removed. The Esquimos have no decided form of religion. When questioned as to where the soul of the good Esquimo will go, they reply by pointing upward; and by pointing downward, the question is answered as to the final dwelling-place of the wicked.

The main cause of death amongst the Esquimos is from a disease the symptoms of which are a cough, nausea, and fever, which disease quickly causes death.

It is true that the Esquimos are of little value to the commercial world, due probably to their isolated position; but these same unlearned and uncivilized people have rendered valuable assistance in the discovery of the North Pole.

ENDNOTES

1. Robert E. Peary, *The North Pole* (New York: Frederick A. Stokes Co., 1910), 20.

2. "Why Bartlett Did Not Get to the Pole," *New York Times,* July 16, 1910, 4.

3. Matthew Alexander Henson, *A Negro Explorer at the North Pole,* with a foreword by Robert E. Peary and an introduction by Booker T. Washington [first edition] (New York: Frederick A. Stokes Co., 1912).

4. *Ibid.,* 188.

5. *Ibid.,* xix and xx.

6. *Ibid.,* 136.

7. Rear Admiral Thomas D. Davies, *Robert E. Peary at the North Pole* (n.p.: Foundation for the Promotion of the Art of Navigation, December 11, 1989, www.pearyhenson.org/dougdavies/pearyEvidence2.htm).

8. Robert M. Bryce, "New Introduction," *A Negro Explorer at the North Pole* (New York: Cooper Square Press, 2001), xxxiv.

9. Angell, 204.

10. Angell, 80.

11. Film/video recording/DVD. [Matthew Henson, Pentagon ceremony.] James Carmichael Evans, assistant secretary of the navy, US Department of the Navy, as master of ceremonies, marking the forty-first anniversary of the discovery of the North Pole. NARA ADC.7884. [1950.]

12. The handwritten documents in the US National Archives, all with Henson's signature, are these: 1896 (letter to Peary, concerning the problematic date of the birth of wife Eva's child and their marital difficulties); November 1898 (to Peary, about caring for dogs); December 16, 1905 (a five-page "diary" from Cape Sheridan); April 14, 1906 (a brief, crumpled note on ice conditions); September 1906 (a letter to Peary, defending himself about a dispute over bread, concluding with "I remain your Obedient Servant").

13. Helene Vetter characterized the pair in this way following her interview in a letter to Lilian Kiel, stenographer, October 6, 1954. In the Frederick Cook Collection, Library of Congress; cited by Robert Bryce, *Cook & Peary: The Polar Controversy* (Mechanicsburg, PA: Stackpole Books, 1997), chapter 26, note 12.

14. Floyd Miller, *Ahdoolo! The Biography of Matthew A. Henson* (New York: Dutton, 1963), 201.

15. *The House of Stokes 1881–1926* (New York: Frederick A. Stokes Co., 1926), 3.

16. Miller, 202. The evidence comes from papers shown to Miller by the Peary family from their archives.

17. Bowdoin College, correspondence of Donald B. MacMillan.

18. Davies, 173.

19. Henson, first edition, 76, 85.

20. *Ibid.*, 72.

21. *Ibid.*, 94.

22. *Ibid.,* 177.

23. *Ibid.,* 4.

24. Robert M. Bryce, *Cook and Peary: The Polar Controversy Resolved* (Mechanicsburg, PA: Stackpole Books, 1997), 26.

25. Bryce, *Negro Explorer,* introduction, xxvi–xvii.

26. [Interview with Matthew Henson conducted by Mr. Coleman] (New York: Fox Movietone News, ca. 1951). This and other moving images can be found at the Peary-Arctic Museum and Arctic Studies Center, Bowdoin College.

27. Donald Kirkley, "Arctic Adventurer." Clipping in The Explorers Club file; source not identified. "Baltimore" is handwritten on the paper. Date is 1947 or 48.

28. Henson's height has been described as five foot seven or eight. His weight when he was healthy varied from 130 to 150 pounds. His thumb was distorted from prolonged use of the dog whip. In illustrations found in juvenile literature, Henson is usually depicted as considerably taller than average, with a powerful build. One might consider these representations as metaphorical.

29. Lyle Dick, *Muskox Land: Ellesmere Island in the Age of Contact.* (Calgary, Alberta: Calgary University Press, 2001), 231–233.

30. Bowdoin College, correspondence of Donald B. Mac-Millan, to John Allen, June 18, 1962.

31. Attempts to identify Captain Childs through the databases at Mystic Seaport reveal no vessels by that name registered in the United States from 1857 to 1900. While no

"Captain Childs" is listed for the years around 1878 in the region of Washington, DC, Baltimore, et cetera, there were at least three masters with that last name in that year.

32. Bowdoin College, correspondence of Donald B. MacMillan.

33. *Ibid.,* from Irene Faunce to MacMillan, December 16, 1964.

34. *Boston American,* 1910 interview.

35. In 1987 Dr. Allen Coulter brought the sons of Peary and Henson to the United States in a well-publicized visit to lay wreaths at their fathers' graves.

36. Bowdoin College, correspondence of Donald B. Mac-Millan, to John Allen, June 18, 1962.

37. Dick, 124. From USNA, RG 401 (1) A, Robert E. Peary Papers, Papers Relating to Arctic Expeditions, 1886–1909, Greenland: Peary Diary 1–16, November 1900.

38. Josephine Diebitsch-Peary, *My Arctic Journal: A Year Among Ice-fields and Eskimos* (New York and Philadelphia: The Contemporary Publishing Company, 1894), 181.

39. *Ibid.,* 37–38.

40. Bryce, *Negro Explorer,* introduction, xxxiv.

41. *Ibid.,* xliv.

42. Kenn Harper, *Give Me My Father's Body* (South Royalton, VT: Steerforth Press, 1986/2000), 30.

43. Russell W. Gibbons "Polar Research Today: The Tragedy of America's Exploited Black Pioneer Polar Explorer Matthew Henson," Frederick A Cook Society Web site, www

.cookpolar.org/henson.htm. Peary Family Papers, October 19, 1910. Passage also quoted in Bryce, *Cook and Peary,* introduction, 442.

44. Bryce, *Cook and Peary,* 90.

45. "Henson a Lecturer," *New York Times,* October 17, 1909, 2.

46. "Matt Henson Tells the Real Story of Peary's Trip to Pole," *Boston American,* July 17, 1910. Included as appendix 3 in [Matthew Henson], *A Negro Explorer at the North Pole: The Autobiography of Matthew Henson* (Montpelier, VT: Invisible Cities Press, 2001), 145–154.

47. Robinson, 249.

48. *Chicago Defender,* February 12, 1910, 3.

49. S. Allen Counter, introduction to *A Negro Explorer at the North Pole: The Autobiography of Matthew Henson* (Montpelier, VT: Invisible Cities Press, 2001), xiv.

50. Bowdoin College, correspondence of Donald B. Mac-Millan, MacMillan's review of Ripley's manuscript, January 1965, 14.

51. *Ibid.,* to John Allen, June 18, 1962.

52. Robinson, 157.

53. A small leather notebook, with typewritten notes, now in the Library of Morgan State University, lists some of the places where Henson spoke, along with a brief history of the North Pole achievement and notes for a speech. Among them were the Harriet Tubman Community Club, Hempstead, Long Island, New York; Bluefield Colored Institute,

Bluefield West Virginia, on April 12; Gary High School, Gary, West Virginia, on April 13; Douglas High School, Huntington, West Virginia on April 14, and Charleston, West Virginia, on April 15, Morgan (?) College, in June 1924.

54. "Matthew Henson Honored," *New York Times,* April 6, 1929, Nl.

55. This and other moving images of Henson can be found in the Bowdoin College collections.

56. Bowdoin College, correspondence of Donald B. MacMillan, between MacMillan and Brooks Leavitt, May 1935.

57. Pauline Knickerbocker Angell, *To the Top of the World: The Story of Peary and Henson* (Chicago: Rand McNally, 1964), 274.

58. www.frontiernet.net/~chollo/articles/m91p14c.htm.

59. Bowdoin College, correspondence of Donald B. MacMillan, to MacMillan, October 9, 1964 from James Havender, brother of the owner of Havender's Monumental Works near Woodlawn Cemetery. The writer had found a picture of a headstone with this inscription. The original gravestone in the Bronx read: "Matthew A. Henson August 8, 1866–March 9, 1955 reached the North Pole with Peary April 6, 1909 Susan Ross died in March 1922." Susan Ross was the mother of Henson's wife, Lucy. Letter to MacMillan, October 9, 1964, from James Havender, brother of the owner of Havender's Monumental Works near Woodlawn Cemetery.

60. Robinson.

61. Angell, 195. Gardiner served as chief shipping clerk

with a large New York textile firm. See also Floyd Miller, *Ahdoolo! The Biography of Matthew A. Henson* (New York: Dutton, 1963), 116, where Gardiner is described as "race-conscious." Miller credits Gardiner with raising Henson's awareness of the significance of his work for "all Negroes."

62. *Ibid.*, 191.

63. *Ibid.*, 195.

64. Robinson, 120.

65. Richard Bushnell, "Matthew A. Henson: Arctic Explorer," *Mariah, The Quarterly Journal of Wilderness Exploration* (December 1976): 70–73, 82.

66. Davies, 176.

67. "5 with Dogs Reach Pole, Beating Peary's Pace," *New York Times,* April 27, 2005, A11. Lighthearted reenactments have also been undertaken by two other persons of African-American ancestry to visit the North Pole. These adventurers were Darryl Roberts, who went by foot ("Adventurer Went Against the Odds to Inspire Others," by Douglas Martin, *New York Times,* April 21, 1990, 25), and, in 2007, Barbara Hillary, who at age seventy-five learned to ski so that she could travel to the pole by that mode of transport.

68. Bowdoin College, correspondence of Donald B. Mac-Millan, to John Allen, December 1, 1946. The letter to John Allen that follows is also in the Bowdoin College collection.

69. Bowdoin College, correspondence of Donald B. Mac-Millan, to Floyd [Miller?], June 20, 1962.

70. *Ibid.*, to Archie Shamblin, April 10, 1969.

71. Angell, 198.

72. While aware of the modern usage styles for the designation of native peoples of the far north, we use the term "Eskimo" to be consistent with, or close to, Matthew Henson's usage and that of historical documents of his day. The current term for the peoples referred to in Henson's narrative would be "Inuit" or variations thereof.

73. Theon Wright, *The Big Nail: The Story of the Cook-Peary Feud* (New York: John Day Company, 1970).

74. "Matthew Henson," *Jinx Magazine,* www.jinxmagazine.com/henson.html. This online magazine of "Worldwide Urban Adventure" is centered physically in Austin, Texas.

75. *African-American Leaders: A Book of Inspiration for Kids.* Series: Really Big Coloring Books. "Compliments of Amtrak in Honor of Black History Month." (St. Louis, MO: N. W. Bell, 2004), 23.

76. Among busts of Matthew Henson, in addition to John LaFarge's work now in The Explorers Club, is a work showing Henson dressed in business attire, by sculptor Masood Warren, in the collection of Frank Minaya y Willmore (pre-1995).

77. *New York Times,* May 12, 1948, 54.

78. Morgan State University has a small notebook, lantern slides used and presumably taken by Matthew Henson, a pair of gloves worn "to and in the discovery of the North Pole"; Henson's camera and case; tools including a saw, awl,

and knife; a plaster mask; a silver trophy presented to Matthew Henson by the Bronx Chamber of Commerce on April 16, 1929, at a ceremony in his home at 901 Grant Avenue, the Bronx ("Matthew Henson Honored," *New York Times,* April 7, 1929, N1); and a small, brown notebook with thirty pages of instructions and diagrams presumably from Peary relating to the d'Urville camp, dating generally from 1899.

79. The painting by Tom Lovell was lent to the Club by Roger Fawcett on behalf of *True Magazine* in 1958.

Bibliography

Prepared by David H. Stam and Deirdre C. Stam

Previous Editions of Matthew Henson's Autobiography (in Chronological Order)

Henson, Matthew Alexander. *A Negro Explorer at the North Pole.* With a foreword by Robert E. Peary and an introduction by Booker T. Washington. New York: Frederick A. Stokes Co., 1912.

———. *A Negro Explorer at the North Pole.* Grand Rapids, MI: Candace Press, 1966.

———. *A Black Explorer at the North Pole: An Autobiographical Report by the Negro Who Conquered the Top of the World with Admiral Robert E. Peary.* With a foreword by Robert E. Peary and an introduction by Booker T. Washington. New York: Walker and Company, 1969.

———. *A Black Explorer at the North Pole.* Introduction to the Bison Book Edition by Susan A. Kaplan. Lincoln: University of Nebraska Press, 1989.

———. *A Negro Explorer at the North Pole.* With a new introduction by Robert M. Bryce, a foreword by Robert E. Peary and a preface by Booker T. Washington. New York: Cooper Square Press, 2001.

———. *A Negro Explorer at the North Pole: The Autobiography of Matthew Henson.* With a new introduction by S. Allen

Counter. Montpelier, VT: Invisible Cities Press, 2001.

———. *A Negro Explorer at the North Pole.* With a foreword by Robert E. Peary and an introduction by Booker T. Washington. Philadelphia: The Press at Toad Hall, D. N. Goodchild, 2007.

———. *A Negro Explorer at the North Pole.* With a foreword by Robert E. Peary and an introduction by Booker T. Washington. N.p.: Dodo Press, 2007.

———. *A Negro Explorer at the North Pole.* With a foreword by Robert E. Peary and an introduction by Booker T. Washington. Charleston, SC: Bibliobazaar, 2007.

———. *A Negro Explorer at the North Pole.* With a foreword by Robert E. Peary and an introduction by Booker T. Washington. Mineola, NY: Dover Publications, 2008.

SELECTED BOOKS AND ARTICLES

"5 with Dogs Reach Pole, Beating Peary's Pace." *New York Times,* April 27, 2005, A11.

Altman, Susan. *Followers of the North Star: Rhymes About African American Heroes, Heroines, and Historical Times.* Chicago: Children's Press, 1993.

Anderson, Madelyn Klein. *Robert E. Peary and the Fight for the North Pole.* New York: F. Watts, 1992.

Angell, Pauline Knickerbocker. *To the Top of the World: The Story of Peary and Henson.* Chicago: Rand McNally, 1964.

Armentrout, David, and Patricia Armentrout. *Matthew Henson: Discover the Life of an American Legend.* Vera Beach, FL: Rourke Pub., 2004.

Baccus, Joan. *The First Man to Reach the North Pole* [Matthew Henson]. [Graphic novel.] Seattle: Baylor Pub., 1983.

Barber, Terry. *Matthew Henson & Robert Peary.* Edmonton, Alberta: Grass Roots Press, 2007.

Bedesky, Baron. *Peary & Henson: The Race to the North Pole.* New York: Crabtree Publishers, 2006.

Black Explorers in the Frozen Farthest North. Baltimore: Herbert M. Frisby Historical Society, 1973.

Bonner, Lin. "Matt Henson: First to Reach the Pole." *Liberty,* July 17, 1926.

Bryce, Robert M., *Cook and Peary: The Polar Controversy Resolved.* Mechanicsburg, PA: Stackpole Books, 1997.

Bushnell, Richard. "Matthew A. Henson, Arctic Explorer." *Mariah, the Quarterly Journal of Wilderness Exploration* (December 1976): 70–73, 82.

Campos, David, "Explorer Matthew Henson: Ten Steps to a 'Constructivist Lesson.'" *Black History Bulletin* 68 (Summer–Fall 2005): 4, 11.

Counter, S. Allen. "The Henson Family." *National Geographic* 174 (September 1988): 414–429.

———. *North Pole Legacy: Black, White, & Eskimo.* Amherst: University of Massachusetts Press, 1991.

Currie, Stephen. "Matthew Henson." In *Polar Explorers.* San Diego: Lucent Books, 2002.

Cutter, Thomas J. "Robert Peary and Matthew Henson at the North Pole." US Naval Institute, Annapolis. *Proceedings* 122:2 (1997): 85.

Davies, Rear Admiral Thomas D. *Robert E. Peary at the North Pole.* N.p.: Foundation for the Promotion of the Art of Navigation, December 11, 1989.

Dick, Lyle. *Muskox Land: Ellesmere Island in the Age of Contact.* Calgary, Alberta: University Press, 2001.

Diebitsch-Peary, Josephine. *My Arctic Journal: A Year Among Ice-fields and Eskimos.* New York and Philadelphia: The Contemporary Publishing Company, 1894.

Doctorow, Edgar Laurence. *Ragtime.* New York: Random House, 1975.

Dolan, Edward F. *Matthew Henson, Black Explorer.* New York: Dodd, Mead, 1979.

Dolan, Sean. *Matthew Henson.* New York: Chelsea Juniors (Chelsea House), 1992.

Evans, Henry S. "Polar Explorer [Matthew Henson]." *The Explorers Journal* [the official quarterly of The Explorers Club] (September 1988): 124–125.

"Events at Pole Told by Henson." *New York Times,* September 14, 1909, 1.

Explorers and Discoverers: Peary and Henson. Educational Research Council of America. Learner-verified. Boston: Allyn and Bacon, 1974.

Ferris, Jeri. *Arctic Explorer: The Story of Matthew Henson.* Minneapolis: Carolrhoda Books, 1989.

———. *Explore: . . . Invitations to Literacy.* New York: Houghton Mifflin, 1997.

"A Final Resting Place for Matthew Henson." *Ebony,* July 1998, 108–111.

Flemming, Claire. "Henson's Mittens." *The Explorers Journal* [the official quarterly of The Explorers Club] (Fall 2002): 40.

Fowler, Robert H. "The Negro Who Went to the Pole with Peary." *American History* [Parts I and II] (April and May 1966) I: 4–11, 52–55; II: 46f.

Gaines, Ann Graham. *Matthew Henson and the North Pole Expedition.* Chanhassen, MN: Child's World, 2001.

Gates, Henry Louis. *The African-American Century: How Black Americans Have Shaped Our Country.* New York: Free Press, 2000.

Gibbons, Russell. "The Tragedy of Matthew Henson; America's Exploited Black Polar Explorer." *Polar Research Today* [Frederick A. Cook Society], http://www.cookpolar.org/henson.htm.

Gilman, Michael. *Matthew Henson: Explorer.* With an introductory essay by Coretta Scott King. Danbury, CT: Chelsea House Publishers, 1988.

———. *Matthew Henson.* Los Angeles: Melrose Square Pub., 1989.

Gleiter, Jan. *Matthew Henson.* Milwaukee: Raintree Children's Books, 1988.

Gleiter, Jan, and Kathleen Thompson. *Maxiu Hansen.* Illustrated by Francis Balistreri. [In Chinese.] Taibei Shi: Lu qiao wen hua shi ye you xian gong si, 1980–1989 [?].

Graves, Charles Parlin. *Matthew A. Henson.* New York: Putnam's, 1971.

Greenfield, Elise, and Jan Spivey Gilchrist. "Matthew Henson (1866–1955)." In *How They Got There: African Americans and the Call of the Sea.* New York: HarperCollins, 2003.

Harper, Kenn. *Give Me My Father's Body.* South Royalton, VT: Steerforth Press, 1986/2000.

Hart, Scott. "Hero of the North Pole." *Coronet,* May 1947, 19–23.

Haskins, James. "Matthew Henson at the Top of the World." In *One More River to Cross: The Stories of Twelve Black Americans.* New York: Scholastic, 1992.

———. *Against All Opposition: Black Explorers in America.* New York: Walker, 2003.

Hawes, Alison. *Arctic Hero: The Story of Matthew Henson.* Oxford, UK: Oxford University Press, 2003.

Hayden, Robert C. "Matthew A. Henson." In *7 African American Scientists.* Frederick, MD: Twenty-first Century Books, 1970.

Henson, Matthew. "A Negro at the North Pole." *World's Work* 4 (1910): 19.

"Henson, a Lecturer." *New York Times,* October 17, 1909, 2.

Herbert, Wally. *The Noose of Laurels: Robert E. Peary and the Race to the North Pole.* New York: Atheneum, 1989.

Hoena, B. A. *Matthew Henson: Arctic Adventurer.* Illustrated by Phil Miller and Charles Barnett III. Mankato, MN: Capstone Press, 2006.

————. *Matthew Henson: Aventurero del Artico.* Mankato, MN: Capstone Press, 2007.

House of Stokes 1881–1926. New York: Frederick A. Stokes Co., 1926.

Hudson, Wade. "Matthew A. Henson." In *Five Brave Explorers.* New York: Scholastic, 1995.

Johnson, Bridget. "Left Out in the Cold." *Boys Life* [Boy Scouts of America] 92:2 (February 2002): 12.

Johnson, Catherine. *Arctic Hero.* Illustrated by Seb Camagajevac. Edinburgh, Scotland: Barrington Stoke, 2008.

Johnson, Dolores. *Onward: A Photobiography of African-American Polar Explorer Matthew Henson.* Washington, DC: National Geographic, 2006.

Johnson, LaVerne C. *Kumi & Chanti Tell the Story of Matthew Henson.* Chicago: Empak Enterprises, 1992.

Kirkley, Donald. "Arctic Adventurer." Clipping in the Explorers Club files; source not identified. "Baltimore" is handwritten on the paper. Date is 1947 or 1948.

Kramer, Candice. *Matthew Henson at the North Pole.* Pelham, NY: Benchmark Education Co., 2004.

The Life of Matthew Henson. New York: Fitzgerald Publishing Co., 1976.

Litwin, Laura Baskes. *Matthew Henson: Co-Discoverer of the North Pole.* Berkeley Heights, NJ: Enslow Publishers, 2001.

MacMillan, Admiral Donald B. "Matthew Henson." *The Explorers Journal* [fiftieth anniversary issue] (Fall 1955): 28–30, 93.

Martin, Douglas. "Adventurer Went Against the Odds to Inspire Others." *New York Times,* April 21, 1990, 25.

"Matt Henson Tells the Real Story of Peary's Trip to Pole." *Boston American,* July 17, 1910. Included in Matthew Henson, *A Negro Explorer at the North Pole: The Autobiography of Matthew Henson.* Montpelier, VT: Invisible Cities Press, 2001, 145–154.

["Matthew Henson."] *Hampton's Magazine,* July 1910, 138.

May, Julian. *Matthew Henson, Co-Discoverer of the North Pole.* Mankato, MN: Creative Educational Society, 1972.

McAfee, D. "The Travail of Matthew Henson." *Phylon* 36 (1979): 407–416.

Miller, Floyd. *Ahdoolo! The Biography of Matthew A. Henson.* New York: Dutton, 1963.

———. "Ahdoolo! The Heroic March of Matthew Henson." *Readers Digest,* February 1963.

Molett, William E. *Robert Peary and Matthew Henson at the North Pole.* Frankfort, KY: Elkhorn Press , 1966.

Moore, Terris. "Charge of Hoax Against Robert E. Peary Examined." *Alpine Journal* 25:57 (1983): 114–123.

Napoli, Donna Jo. *North.* New York: Greenwillow Books, 2004.

[Obituary for Matthew Henson.] *New York Herald Tribune,* March 10, 1955.

Olmstead, Kathleen. *Matthew Henson: The Quest for the North Pole.* New York: Sterling Pub., 2008.

Peary, Robert E. *The North Pole.* New York: Frederick A. Stokes Co., 1910.

Reef, Catherine. "Matthew Henson." In *Black Explorers*. New York: Facts on File, 2006.

"Remembering Matthew Henson." *New York Times,* July 10, 1936, I8.

Rennett, Richard Scott. "Matthew Henson." In *Pioneers of Discovery*. Series: Profiles of Great Black Americans. New York: Chelsea House, 1994.

Ripley, Sheldon N. *Matthew Henson, Arctic Hero*. Boston: Houghton Mifflin, 1966.

Robinson, Bradley. *Dark Companion*. New York: R. M. McBride, 1947.

———. *Mwenzi mwaminifu, motto Mweusi Maskini ambaye alifku halafu kwenye ncha ya kaskazini*. [In Swahili; abridgement of *Dark Companion*.] London and New York: Longmans, Green, 1950.

———. "Matthew A. Henson, 1866–1955." *Arctic, Journal of the Arctic Institute of North America* (March 1983): 106–107.

Rozakis, Laurie. *Matthew Henson & Robert Peary: The Race for the Pole*. Woodbridge, CT: Blackbirch Press, 1994.

Sanger, Richard. *Two Words for Snow*. [Play by Richard Sanger with Matthew Henson as central character.] Calgary, Alberta: Red Deer Press, 2005.

Schlesinger, Arthur M. *Robert E. Peary and the Rush to the North Pole: Chronicles from National Geographic*. Philadelphia: Chelsea House Publishers, 1999.

Schraff, Anne E. "Matthew Henson and Robert Peary." *American Heroes of Exploration and Flight.* Springfield, NJ: Enslow Pubs., 1996.

Sherman, Josepha. *Exploring the North Pole: The Story of Robert Edwin Peary and Matthew Henson.* Hockessin, DE: Mitchell Lane, 2006.

Thomas, Lowell. "First at the Pole." [Publication describing interview with Matthew Henson.] *Lowell Thomas Interviews,* April 2, 1939.

Weatherford, Carole Boston, and Eric Velasquez. *I, Matthew Henson: Polar Explorer.* New York: Walker, 2008.

Weidt, Maryann N. *Matthew Henson.* Illustrated by Tim Parlin. New York: Backpack Books, 2002.

———. *Matthew Henson.* Minneapolis: Lerner Publications, 2003.

"Why Bartlett Did Not Get to the Pole." *New York Times,* July 16, 1910, 4.

Williams, Jean Kinney. *Matthew Henson, Polar Adventurer.* New York: Franklin Watts, 1994.

Wright, Theon. *The Big Nail: The Story of the Cook-Peary Feud.* New York: John Day Company, 1970.

AUDIOVISUAL MEDIA

Film/video recording/DVD. *Beyond the Pole: USNS* Matthew Henson. Describes the US Naval Ship *Henson;* also chronicles the life of Henson. Starkville: Mississippi State University Television Center, 1998.

Film/video recording/DVD. [Biography of Matthew Henson.] Ralph Kendall Berge, producer. Made for cable television (Turner Broadcasting System, ca. 1998). Hawthorne, CA: Close Out Movies, 1907.

Film/video recording/DVD. [Interview with Matthew Henson by Mr. Coleman.] Possibly for TV. New York: Fox Movietone News, ca. 1951.

Film/video recording/DVD. *Matthew Henson, Explorer.* Michael Gilman. Series: Black Americans of Achievement. Duration: 30 minutes. Balalynwyd, PA: Schlessinger Video Productions, 1994.

Film/video recording/DVD. [Matthew Henson, Pentagon ceremony.] James Carmichael Evans, assistant secretary of the navy, US Department of the Navy, as master of ceremonies, marking the forty-first anniversary of the discovery of the North Pole. General Ginsberg reads a message from President Truman. Also includes a message from Admiral Byrd. The leader incorrectly identifies the film as honoring Byrd. Henson begins reading a response but is unable to continue, overcome by emotion. The film ends prematurely due to technical difficulty. Copy: NARA ADC.7884. [1950.]

Film/video recording/DVD. *North Pole Legacy: Black, White and Eskimo.* Dr. S. Allen Counter, producer and director. Duration: 56 minutes. Champaign: Illinois Video, 1987 John

Palmer; S. Allen Counter, authors. Etna, NH: Distributed by the Nabby Dodge Corp., EcoVideo, 1999, ca. 1996.

Film/video recording/DVD. *Peary and Henson: North to the Pole.* Duration: 15 minutes. New York: McGraw-Hill Book Company, Project 7 Productions, 1969.

Film strip. "Robert Peary and Matthew Henson." Burton M. Munk, author; Felix Palm, illustrator. Chicago: Society for Visual Education Inc., 1978.

Radio play. [Matthew Henson.] Maker/distributor: US Armed Forces Radio and Television Service. RG 330.AFRTS 1138. 1955.

Radio program/audiotape. [Matthew Alexander Henson, 1866–1955.] Richard Durham, scriptwriter. Series: Destination Freedom: Harriet's Children. Duration: 30 minutes. Maker/distributor: Chicago: WMAQ, 1949.

Video recording/teleplay. *Glory and Honor.* Teleplay by Jeffrey Lewes and Susan Rhinehart, based on a story by Robert Caputo. Burbank, CA: Warner Home Video, 1997/1998. Related materials: (1) "Glory and Honor: Press Materials." Including 33 mm slides. TNT Original. (2) Poster. Issued with "education grade materials." 1999.

COLLECTIBLES/MULTIPLES

Bust of Henson, depicting Henson's head with fur hood. Thomas Blackshear II, artist. Series: Proud Heritage Collection. Material: Crushed pecan shells and resin, handpainted. Size: 8.75 inches. Distributor: Glencoe, AL: Miss Martha Originals [Martha Holcome Root], ca. 1995–2000.

Bust of Henson, depicting Henson bareheaded with beard. Material: Bronzelike, probably plastic. Color: Gray-brown. Size: About 10 inches high. Created for a commercial promotion. Maker/distributor: Old Taylor [bourbon company], 1969.

Ceramic plate, with large image of Henson's head with fur hood, small-scale Eskimo companions in foreground. Thomas Blackshear II, artist. In color. Series: Legacy of Courage: Proud Heritage Collection. Size: 8 inches in diameter. Distributor: Glencoe, AL: Miss Martha Originals [Martha Holcome Root], 1995.

Ceramic plate, with image of Henson's head with fur hood, reproduced from photograph. In black and white, with gold edge. Size: 8 inches in diameter. No identifying information on piece.

Ceremonial bronze coin, depicting the race to the North Pole, 1909. Reverse: description of the major historical events of 1909. Mint stamped and numbered on smooth edge. Weight: 1.2 ounces. Maker: Franklin Mint.

Decorative magnet. "Peary-MacMillan Arctic Museum, Brunswick, Maine." Bears the image of the 22-cent US postage stamp depicting Peary and Henson from 1986. Material: plastic sheet, with magnet affixed to the back. Size: 1.75 inches high x 2 inches. Maker/distributor: Brunswick, ME: Peary-MacMillan Arctic Museum.

Game [boxed set]. The Black Explorers: Math Adventure Game. Includes Henson as one of four subjects. Ca. 1990. Educational game/activity set. Includes booklet, figures of Peary and Henson, sledge, dogs, and igloo. Material: plastic, in color. Size of container: 14 inches high x 11.5 inches. Maker/distributor: Montpelier, VT: Child Light LLC, 2000.

Envelope, depicting Henson and Peary (head shots) with dog team in foreground. Distributed with actual Peary-Henson stamp of 1986 affixed. Printed on recto: "First Day of Issue." Postmark from "North Pole AK May 28 1986 99705." Maker/distributor: Fleetwood, 1986.

Figurine of Matthew Henson. "Matthew Henson, America's Resourceful Explorer 1866–1955." Series: Trailblazer. Fully posable action figure, with separate sextant, snowshoes, ice ax, goggles, and ice anchor. Material: colored plastic. Size: box is 9 inches high x 6.5 inches; figurine is 6.5 inches high. Maker/distributor: Washington DC: HIA [History in Action] Toys, ca. 2000 or later.

Figurine of Matthew Henson. Full, standing figure in furs with flag and dog. Series: All God's Children. Material: painted plaster (?). Size: 5.25 inches high x 5.5 inches. Maker/

distributor: Glencoe, AL: Miss Martha Originals, ca. 2003.

"Long penny," depicting head of Matthew Henson. Text impressed around the image: "Matthew A. Henson, Arctic Explorer." Vertical orientation. [A "long penny" is made from US coinage; the coin is rolled through a press, and in the process an image is affixed to the elongated form.] Maker/distributor: Long Penny Mercantile Collection.

Postage stamp, with head shot of Peary and Henson dressed in furs; part of a set of four, all depicting explorers. Face value: 22 cents. Maker: US Postal Service, 1986.

Poster, depicting Matthew Henson, dressed in furs, shading his eyes with gloved hand, looking to the viewer's left; design includes ship and other details with some text in upper corner. Color. Vertical orientation. Size: ca. 20 inches high x 17 inches.

Postcard, depicting Matthew Henson and Robert Peary. Design on recto includes color photograph of the 22-cent Peary-Henson stamp issued in 1986, accompanied by text below. Verso: "Matthew Alexander Henson 1966–1955." Size: 7 inches recto height x 5 inches. Maker/distributor: US Postal Service, US Allegiance Inc., 1986.

Postcard, depicting Matthew Henson in furs with bare head; upper torso and head. Black and white. From postcard book. Recto: vertical orientation. Size: 6.5 inches high x 4.75 inches. Maker/distributor: Pomegranate Art Book, 1989.

Print, depicting a collage of Henson-related images and texts. Color. Size: ca. 9 inches high x 12 inches. Original from ca.

1980. Revised edition reissued by Verne Robinson, ca. 2000 or later.

Puzzle. Giant-size "floor puzzle" of Matthew Henson with a brief biography of Henson on the box. Series: Black Heritage. Material: cardboard. 24 pieces. Size: 33 inches high x 24 inches. Maker/distributor: Geebee Marketing Inc.

Trade card, depicting Henson on the front, with a brief biography on verso. Size: 6 inches high x 4 inches. Maker/distributor: Grolier Inc., 1997.

Trade card. "Matthew Henson: The World's Greatest Explorer." Size: 3 inches high x 2.75 inches. Albert Operti, artist. In color. Marker/distributor: New York: Hassan Cork Tip Cigarettes, n.d. [probably shortly after 1909].

THE EXPLORERS CLUB

HISTORY AND MISSION STATEMENT

Founded in 1904, The Explorers Club is a multidisciplinary, professional society dedicated to the advancement of field research, scientific exploration, and the ideal that it is vital to preserve the instinct to explore. The overall mission of the Club is the encouragement of scientific exploration of land, sea, air, and space, with particular emphasis on the physical and biological sciences. The headquarters for the worldwide activities of The Explorers Club and its Chapters is the landmark Lowell Thomas Building on East 70th Street in New York City.

The Club is international in scope, with 3,500 members representing every continent and more than sixty countries. Over the years, membership has included polar explorers Roald Amundsen, Robert E. Peary, Matthew Henson, Ernest Shackleton, and Richard C. Byrd; aviators James Doolittle, Charles Lindbergh, and Chuck Yeager; underwater pioneers Sylvia Earle, Jacques Piccard, Don Walsh, and Robert Ballard; astronauts John Glenn, Buzz Aldrin, Neil Armstrong, Sally Ride, and Kathryn Sullivan, and cosmonaut Viktor Savinykh; anthropologists Louis Leakey, Richard Leakey, and Jane Goodall; mountaineers Sir Edmund Hillary and Tenzing

Norgay; former US presidents Theodore Roosevelt and Herbert Hoover; and other notables, including journalist Lowell Thomas, explorer-anthropologist Thor Heyerdahl, and biologist Dr. James Watson.

The Explorers Club is a gathering place and unifying force for explorers and field scientists the world over, serving as a base for expedition planning, presentations, meetings, and events. The Club's library and archives holds an unparalleled collection of exploration-related literature, documents, and artifacts. Its unique grant programs provide funding to undergraduate and graduate students who are pursuing field research around the globe.

Today, the importance of The Explorers Club's mission remains as powerful as ever: to be a wellspring for the impulse to explore and to serve as a stimulus for the enduring spirit of exploration and scientific inquiry in human life.

For more information on The Explorers Club, go to www.explorers.org.